THE RAILWAY BRIDGE
OF THE SILVERY TAY
AND OTHER DISASTERS

Selected from the works of
William McGonagall

Born in Dundee in 1830, William
McGonagall came to the attention of the
literary world by an unusual route. During
his lifetime he wrote hundreds of poems—
unanimously reckoned the worst poetry
ever published! Nonetheless, McGonagall
is widely read, his immortally execrable
verse enjoyed by thousands of devotees.
This volume contains the best—or worst—
of the Scottish 'poet and tragedian',
including such immortal gems as THE
RAILWAY BRIDGE OF THE
SILVERY TAY, GREENLAND'S ICY
MOUNTAINS and THE HORRORS OF
MAJUBA. William McGonagall died in
Edinburgh in 1902.

THE RAILWAY BRIDGE
OF THE SILVERY TAY
AND OTHER DISASTERS

The Railway Bridge of the Silvery Tay and Other Disasters

Selected from the works of
WILLIAM McGONAGALL
Poet and Tragedian, Died in Edinburgh
29th September, 1902

SPHERE BOOKS LIMITED
30/32 Gray's Inn Road, London, WC1X 8JL

First published in Great Britain
by David Winter & Son Ltd.
© David Winter & Son Ltd. and the Corporation of Dundee
First Sphere Books edition 1972

Printed in Great Britain by
Hazell Watson & Viney Ltd,
Aylesbury, Bucks

CONTENTS

CONTENTS (contd.)

A SUMMARY HISTORY OF POET McGONAGALL

Poet McGonagall was born In the Month of March 1825. His parents were Irish and his Father left Ireland, shortly after His marriage and came to Scotland. And got settled down In Ayrshire In a place call'd Maybole as a Cotton Weaver, and lived there for About ten years untill the Cotton Weaving began to fail there, and Then he was Induced to leave it owing to the very small demand There was for Cotton weaving In that part of Scotland. Then he and his family left Maybole, and came to Edinburgh Where he got settled down again to work Cotton fabrics which there was a greater demand for, than in Maybole, and by this time they family consisted of two Sons, And three daughters. William, The Poet, was the youngest, and was born in Edinburgh. And the rest of the family was born in Maybole And Dundee. his Father lived in Edinburgh for more than eight years, untill the Cotton Weaving began to fail, then his Father and they family left Edinburgh, And travelled to the Orkney Isles, And to a house for they family to live in the Island of Southronaldsay And his father bought the Living as a Pedlar, and supported the family by selling hardware, among they peasantry In the Orkney Isles, and returning home every night to his family, when circumstances would permit him. Charles the eldest son was herding Cows to a Farmer in the Island of South-ronaldsay, and his eldest Sister Nancy, was in the service of a Farmer in the same locality, and William, the Poet, and Thomas, the second eldest brother, was sent to School to be teached by Mr. James Forbes, the parish Schoolmaster, Who was a very Strict Dominie indeed, of which our readers shall hear of as a proof of his strictness, a rather curious incident. William, the Poet, chanced to be one day in his garden behind the school, and Chanc'd to espy a live,

Tortoise, that the Dominie kept in the garden, and never having seen such a curious kind of a reptile before, his Curiousity was therefore excited no doubt to see it, and he stooped down and lifted the Tortoise with both hands, thereon admiring the varied beautiful Colours of its shell. when behold it dunged upon both hands of William the poet, which was rather aggravating to William, no doubt, and he dash'd the Tortoise on the ground which almost killed it. And the Dominie Chanc'd to see him, at the time through the back window of the Schoolroom, and he rattled on the window with his Cane to William, which startled him, and as soon as William came in to the School, he layd hold on him and began to beat him unmercifully about the body and face, untill his face was blackened in many places, with his hard Taws. and persisted in it untill some of the elder Scholars cried out to him to Stop! beating William. and when William went home to his dinner, and told his father all about it as it had happened his father flew into a rage and said he would be revenged upon him for beating William so unmerciful, and accordingly he went to a Magistrate, with William, and related the Case to him as it had happened. and when the Magistrate examined Williams face, and seen the marks, the Dominie had left thereon he ask'd Williams father if he was willing to put him from ever being a Schoolmaster in the parish again, but Williams Father would not consent to hear of that owing to the Kindness he had shown towards his Son, Thomas, and he simply ask'd the Magistrate, to give him a line, to certify, to Mr. Forbes, that he could put him from ever being a Schoolmaster in that parish again if he would just say the word. so Williams Father went with him to the Dominie, and showed him the line he had got from the Magistrate, to certify that he could put him from being a Schoolmaster again in the parish if he would say the word. and when the Dominie read he was very much surprised and began to make an Apology to Williams Father for what he had done, and promised he would never do the like again. so William and his Father were well satisfied for getting such a sweet revenge, upon that Dominie, and ever after that William was a great favourite of the Dominies and just acted as he pleased and was always very unwilling to go to School. Williams Father had to beat him very often before he would go to School, so that he never got a very great share of education.

William has been like the Immortal Shakespeare he had learn'd more from nature than ever he learn'd at School. William has been from his boyhood a great admirer of every thing that is Considered to be beautiful such as beautiful Rivers and mountain Scenery and beautiful landscapes, and great men such as Shakespeare and great preachers, such as the Rev. George Gilfillan, and Great Poets such as Burns, or Tanna'hill, and Campbell &c. but again I must return to Williams Father he stay'd in the Island of Southronaldsay for about three years, and then left it with the Family, and came to Dundee, and settled down in it. and those of the family that were able to work were sent to the Mills and some of his Sons wrought at the handloom in the Factory along with himself, that was Thomas, and Charles, and William wrought in the Mill for a few years. and then his Father took him from the Mill, and learnd him the handloom himself and he has followed that occupation up to the present when he Can get it to do. he has always had a great liking for Theatrical representation and has made several appearances upon the Stage, In the Theatre Royal Dundee, In the Character of Macbeth, under the Management of Mr. Caple. he has also play'd the Characters of Hamlet and Othello, Macbeth, and Richard III, In the Music Hall under the Management of Forrest Knowles, to delighted and crowded audiences. and it is only recently ago that he discovered himself to be a poet. the desire for writing Poetry came upon him In the Month of June 1877 that he could not resist the desire for writing poetry the first piece he wrote was An Address to the Rev. George Gilfillan, to the Weekly News, only giving the Initials of his name, W. M. G. Dundee which was received with eclat, then he turned his muse to the Tay Bridge, and sung it successfully and was pronounced by the press the Poet Laureate of The Tay Bridge then he unfolded himself

13

to they public, and honestly gave out to them his own name. then he wrote an Address to Robert Burns. Also upon Shakspeare, which he sent printed Copies of to her Majesty, and received her Royal Patronage for so doing. he has also Composed the following effusions, the Bonnie broon haird Lassie o' Bonnie Dundee, and A Companion to it Little Jeemie, also the Convicts return home again to Scotland and the Silvery Tay, and a host of others to numerous to mention, which will be publish'd shortly.

© *The Corporation of Dundee*

BRIEF AUTOBIOGRAPHY

DEAR READER,—My parents were both born in Ireland, where they spent the great part of their lives after their marriage. They left Ireland for Scotland, and never returned to the Green Isle. I was born in the year 1830 in the city of Edinburgh, the garden of bonnie Scotland, which is justly famed for all its magnificent scenery. My parents were poor, but honest, sober, and God-fearing. My father was a hand-loom weaver, and wrought at cotton fabrics during his stay in Edinburgh, which was for about two years. Owing to the great depression in the cotton trade in Edinburgh, he removed to Paisley with his family, where work was abundant for a period of about three years; but then a crash taking place, he was forced to remove to Glasgow with his family with the hope of securing work there, and enable him to support his young and increasing family, as they were all young at the time, your humble servant included. In Glasgow he was fortunate in getting work as a cotton weaver; and as trade was in a prosperous state for about two years, I was sent to school, where I remained about eighteen months, but at the expiry of which, trade again becoming dull, my poor parents were compelled to take me from school, being unable to pay for schooling through adverse circumstances; so that all the education I received was before I was seven years of age.

My father, being forced to leave Glasgow through want of work, came to Dundee, where plenty of work was to be had at the time—such as sacking, cloth, and other fabrics. It was at this time that your humble servant was sent to work in a mill in the Scouringburn, which was owned by Mr Peter Davie, and there I remained for about four years, after which I was taken from the mill, and put to learn the hand-loom in Ex-Provost Reid's factory, which was also situated in the Scouringburn. After I had learned to be an expert hand-loom weaver, I began to take a great delight in reading books, as well as to improve my handwriting, in my leisure hours at night, until I made myself what I am.

The books that I liked best to read were Shakspeare's penny plays, more especially Macbeth, Richard III, Hamlet, and Othello; and I gave myself no rest until I obtained complete mastery over the above four characters. Many a time in my dear father's absence I enacted entire scenes from Macbeth and Richard III, along with some of my shopmates, until they were quite delighted; and many a time they regaled me and the other actors that had entertained them to strong ale, biscuits, and cheese.

My first appearance on any stage was in Mr Giles' theatre, which was in Lindsay Street quarry, some years ago : I cannot give the exact date, but it is a very long time ago. The theatre was built of brick, somewhat similar to Mr McGivern's at the top of Seagate. The character that I appeared in was Macbeth, Mrs Giles sustaining the character of Lady Macbeth on that occasion, which she performed admirably. The way that I was allowed to perform was in terms of the following agreement, which was entered into between Mr Giles and myself—that I had to give Mr Giles one pound in cash before the performance, which I considered rather hard, but as there was no help for it, I made known Mr Giles' terms to my shopmates, who were hand-loom weavers in Seafield Works, Taylor's Lane. No sooner than the terms were made known to them, than they entered heartily into the arrangement, and in a very short time they made up the pound by subscription, and with one accord declared they would go and see me perform the Thane of Fife, *alias* Macbeth. To see that the arrangement with Mr Giles was carried out to the letter, a deputation of two of my shopmates was appointed to wait upon him with the pound. Mr Giles received the deputation, and on receipt of the money cheerfully gave a written agreement certifying that he would allow me to perform Macbeth on the following night in his theatre. When the deputation came back with the news that Mr Giles had consented to allow me to make my *debut* on the following night, my shopmates cheered again and again, and the rapping of the lays I will never forget as long as I live. When the great night arrived my shopmates were in high glee with the hope of getting a Shakspearian treat from your humble servant. And I can assure you, without boasting, they were not disappointed in their anticipations, my shopmates having secured seats before the general public were admitted. It would be impossible for me to describe the scene in Lindsay Street, as it was crowded from head to foot, all being eager to witness my first appearance as an exponent of Shakspeare. When I appeared on the stage I was received with a perfect storm of applause, but when I exclaimed "Command, they make a halt upon the heath," the applause was deafening, and was continued during the entire evening, especially so in the combat scene. The house was crowded during each of the three performances on that ever-memorable night, which can never be forgot by me or my shopmates, and even entire strangers included. At the end of each performance I was called before the curtain, and received plaudit after plaudit of applause in recognition of my able impersonation of Macbeth.

What a sight it was to see such a mass of people struggling to gain admission! hundreds failing to do so, and in the struggle numbers were trampled under foot, one man having lost one of his shoes in the scrimmage; others were carried bodily into the theatre along with the press. So much then for the true account of my first appearance on any stage.

The most startling incident in my life was the time I discovered myself to be a poet, which was in the year 1877. During the Dundee holiday week, in the bright and balmy month of June, when trees and flowers were in full bloom, when lonely and sad in my room, I sat thinking about the thousands of people who were away by rail and steamboat, perhaps to the land of Burns, or poor ill-treated Tannahill, or to gaze upon the Trossachs in Rob Roy's country, or elsewhere wherever their minds led them. Well, while pondering so, I seemed to feel as it were a strange kind of feeling stealing over me, and remained so for about five minutes. A flame, as Lord Byron has said, seemed to kindle up my entire frame, along with a strong desire to write poetry; and I felt so happy, so happy, that I was inclined to dance, then I began to pace backwards and forwards in the room, trying to shake off all thought of writing poetry; but the more I tried, the more strong the sensation became. It was so strong, I imagined that a pen was in my right hand, and a voice crying, "Write Write!" So I said to myself, ruminating, let me see; what shall I write? then all at once a bright idea struck me to write about my best friend, the late Reverend George Gilfillan; in my opinion I could not have chosen a better subject, therefore I immediately found paper, pen, and ink, and set myself down to immortalize the great preacher, poet, and orator. These are the lines I penned, which I dropped into the box of the *Weekly News* office surreptitiously, which appeared in that paper as follows :—

"W. M'G., Dundee, who modestly seeks to hide his light under a bushel, has surreptitiously dropped into our letter-box an address to the Rev. George Gilfillan. Here is a sample of this worthy's powers of versification :

'Rev. George Gilfillan of Dundee,
  There is none can you excel;
You have boldly rejected the Confession of Faith,
  And defended your cause right well.

'The first time I heard him speak,
  'Twas in the Kinnaird Hall,
Lecturing on the Garibaldi movement,
  As loud as he could bawl.

'He is a liberal gentleman
  To the poor while in distress,
And for his kindness unto them
  The Lord will surely bless.

18

'My blessing on his noble form,
    And on his lofty head,
May all good angels guard him while living,
    And hereafter when he's dead.' "

P.S.—This is the first poem that I composed while under
the divine inspiration, and is true, as I have to give an
account to God at the day of judgment for all the sins I
have committed.

With regard to my far-famed Balmoral journey, I will
relate it truly as it happened. 'Twas on a bright summer
morning in the month of July 1878, I left Dundee *en route*
for Balmoral, the Highland home of Her Most Gracious
Majesty, Queen of Great Britain and Empress of India.
Well, my first stage for the day was the village of Alyth.
When I arrived there I felt weary, foot-sore, and longed
for rest and lodgings for the night. I made enquiry for a
good lodging-house, and found one very easily, and for the
lodging I paid fourpence to the landlady before I sat
down, and when I had rested my weary limbs for about
five minutes I rose and went out to purchase some pro-
visions for my supper and breakfast—some bread, tea,
sugar, and butter— and when I had purchased the pro-
visions I returned to my lodgings and prepared for myself
a hearty tea, which I relished very much, I can assure you,
for I felt very hungry, not having tasted food of any kind
by the way during the travel, which caused me to have a
ravenous appetite, and to devour it greedily; and after
supper I asked the landlady to oblige me with some water
to wash my feet, which she immediately and most cheer-
fully supplied me with; then I washed my sore blistered
feet and went to bed, and was soon in the arms of Mor-
pheus, the god of sleep. Soundly I slept all the night, until
the landlady awoke me in the morning, telling me it was a
fine sunshiny morning. Well, of course I rose, and donned
my clothes, and I felt quite refreshed after the refreshing
sleep I had got during the night; then I gave myself a good
washing, and afterwards prepared my breakfast, which I
devoured quickly, and left the lodging-house, bidding the

landlady good morning, and thanking her for her kindness; then I wended my way the next day as far as the Spittal o' Glenshee.

And, my dear friends, when I arrived at the Spittal o' Glenshee, a dreadful thunder-storm came on, and the vivid flashes of the forked lightning were fearful to behold, and the rain poured down in torrents, until I was drenched to the skin, and longed to be under cover from the pitiless rain. Still God gave me courage to proceed on my weary journey, until I arrived at a shepherd's house near by the wayside, and I called at the house, as God had directed me to do, and knocked at the door fearlessly. I was answered by the servant maid, who asked me kindly what I wanted, and I told her that I wanted lodgings for the night, and that I was wet to the skin with the rain, and that I felt cold and hungry, and that I would feel thankful for any kind of shelter for the night, as it was still raining and likely to be for the night. Then she told me there was no accommodation; then the shepherd himself came to the door, and asked me what I wanted, and I told him I wanted a lodging for the night, and at first he seemed unwilling, eyeing me with a suspicious look, perhaps taking me for a burglar, or a sheep-stealer, who had come to steal his sheep—at least that was my impression. But when I showed him Her Most Gracious Majesty's royal letter, with the royal black seal, that I had received from her for my poetic abilities, he immediately took me by the hand and bade me come in, and told me to "gang in ower to the fire and to warm mysel'," at the same time bidding the servant girl make some porridge ready for the poet; and while the servant girl was making some porridge for me, I showed him a copy of my poems, which I gave to him as a present for his kindness towards me, which he read during the time I was taking my supper, and seemed to appreciate very much. Then when I had taken my supper, he asked me if I would be afraid to sleep in the barn, and I told him so long as I put my trust in God I had nought to fear, and that these were the principles my dear parents had taught me. When I told him so he felt quite delighted, and bade me warm my feet before I would "gang out to my bed i' the barn," and when I had warmed my feet, he accompanied me to the barn, where there was a bed that might have pleased Her Most Gracious Majesty, and rolling down the bed-clothes with his own hands, he wished me a sound sleep, and bade me good night. Then I instantly undressed and tumbled into bed, and was soon sound asleep, dreaming that I saw Her Most Gracious Majesty riding in her carriage-and-pair, which was afterwards truly verified. Well, when I awoke the next morning I felt rather chilled, owing to the wetting I had got, and the fatigue of the distance I had travelled; but, nothing daunted, I still resolved to see Her Majesty. So I dressed myself quickly, and went over to the house to bid the shepherd good morning, and thank him for the kindness I had received at his hands, but I was told by the girl he was away tending the sheep, but that he had told her to give me my breakfast, and she bade me come in and sit down and get it. So of course I went in, and got a good breakfast of porridge and good Highland milk, enough to make a hungry soul to sing with joy, especially in a strange country, and far from home. Well, having breakfasted, I arose and bade the servant girl good-bye, at the same time thanking her and the shepherd—her master—for their kindness towards me. Then, taking to the road again, I soon came in sight of the Castleton o' Braemar, with its beautiful whitewashed houses and romantic scenery, which I have referred to in my poem. When I arrived at the Castleton o' Braemar it was near twelve o'clock noon, and from the Castleton it is twelve miles to Balmoral; and I arrived at the lodge gates of the palace of Balmoral just as the tower clock chimed three; and when I crossed the little bridge that spans the river Dee, which had been erected by Her Majesty, I walked boldly forward and knocked loudly at the porter lodge door, and it was immediately answered by the two constables that are there night and day, and one of them asked me in a very authoritative tone what I wanted, and of course I told him I wanted to see Her Majesty, and he repeated, "Who do you want to see?"

and I said I was surprised to think that he should ask me again after telling him distinctly that I wanted to see Her Majesty. Then I showed him Her Majesty's royal letter of patronage for my poetic abilities, and he read it, and said it was not Her Majesty's letter; and I said "Who's is it then? do you take me for a forger?" Then he said Sir Thomas Biddulph's signature was not on the letter, but I told him it was on the envelope, and he looked and found it to be so. Then he said, "Why didn't you tell me that before?" I said I forgot. Then he asked me what I wished him to do with the letter, and I requested him to show it to Her Majesty or Sir Thomas Biddulph. He left me, pretending to go up to the palace with the letter, standing out in the cold in front of the lodge, wondering if he would go up to the palace as he pretended. However, be that as it may, I know not, but he returned with an answer as follows :—"Well, I've been up at the Castle with your letter, and the answer I got for you is they cannot be bothered with you," said with great vehemence. "Well," I replied, "it cannot be helped"; and he said it could not, and began to question me when I left Dundee, and the way I had come from Dundee, and where I had lodged by the way; and I told him, and he noted it all down in his memorandum book, and when he had done so he told me I would have to go back home again the same way I came; and then he asked me if I had brought any of my poetry with me, and I said I had, and showed him the second edition, of which I had several copies, and he looked at the front of it, which seemed to arrest his attention, and said, "You are not poet to Her Majesty; Tennyson's the real poet to Her Majesty." Then I said, "Granted; but, sir, you cannot deny that I have received Her Majesty's patronage." Then he said, "I should like very well to hear you give some specimens of your abilities," and I said, "Where?" and he said, "Just where you stand"; and I said, "No, sir, nothing so degrading in the open air. When I give specimens of my abilities it is either in a theatre or some hall, and if you want to hear me take me inside of the lodge, and pay me before I begin;

22

then you shall hear me. These are my conditions, sir; do you accpt my terms?" Then he said, "Oh, you might to oblige the young lady there." So I looked around to see the young lady he referred to, and there she was, looking out at the lodge entrance; and when I saw her I said, "No, sir, I will not; if it were Her Majesty's request I wouldn't do it in the open air, far less do it to please the young lady." Then the lady shut the lodge door, and he said, "Well, what do you charge for this book of poems?" and I said "2d.'" and he gave it to me, telling me to go straight home and not to think of coming back again to Balmoral. So I bade him good-bye and retraced my steps in search of a lodging for the night, which I obtained at the first farmhouse I called at; and when I knocked at the door I was told to come in and warm my feet at the fire, which I accordingly did, and when I told the good wife and man who I was, and about me being at the palace, they felt very much for me, and lodged me for the night, and fed me likewise, telling me to stay with them for a day or two, and go to the roadside and watch Her Majesty, and speak to her, and that I might be sure she would do something for me, but I paid no heed to their advice. And when I got my supper, I was shown out to the barn by the gudeman, and there was prepared for me a bed which might have done a prince, and the gudeman bade me good night. So I closed the barn door and went to bed, resolving to be up very early the next morning and on the road, and with the thought thereof I couldn't sleep. So as soon as daylight appeared, I got up and donned my clothes, and went to the farmer's door and knocked, for they had not arisen, it being so early, and I bade them good-bye, thanking them at the same time for their kindness; and in a few minutes I was on the road again for Dundee—it being Thursday morning I refer to—and lodging in the same houses on my homeward journey, which I accomplished in three days, by arriving in Dundee on Saturday early in the day, foot-sore and weary, but not the least discouraged. So ends my ever-memorable journey to Balmoral.

My next adventure was going to New York, America, in the year 1887, March the 10th. I left Glasgow on board the beautiful steamer "Circassia," and had a very pleasant voyage for a fortnight at sea; and while at sea I was quite a favourite amongst the passengers, and displayed my histrionic abilities, to the delight of the passengers, but received no remuneration for so doing; but I was well pleased with the diet I received; also with the kind treatment I met with from the captain and chief steward—Mr Hendry. When I arrived at Castle Garden, New York, I wasn't permitted to pass on to my place of destination until the officials there questioned me regarding the place in New York I was going to, and how old I was, and what trade I was; and, of course, I told them I was a weaver, whereas if I had said I was a poet, they wouldn't have allowed me to pass, but I satisfied them in their interrogations, and was allowed to pass on to my place of destination. During my stay in New York with a Dundee man, I tried occasionally to get an engagement from theatrical proprietors and music-hall proprietors, but alas! 'twas all in vain, for they all told me they didn't encourage rivalry, but if I had the money to secure a hall to display my abilities, or a company of my own, I would make lots of money; but I am sorry to say I had neither, therefore I considered wisely it was time to leave, so I wrote home to a Dundee gentleman requesting him to take me home, and he granted my request cheerfully, and secured for me a passage on board the "Circassia" again, and I had a very pleasant return voyage home again to bonnie Dundee. Since I came home to Dundee I have been very well treated by the more civilised community, and have made several appearances before the public in Baron Zeigler's circus and Transfield's circus, to delighted and crowded audiences; and the more that I was treated unkindly by a few ignorant boys and the Magistrates of the city, nevertheless my heart still clings to Dundee; and, while in Glasgow, my thoughts, night and day, were always towards Dundee; yet I must confess, during a month's stay in Glasgow, I gave three private entertainments to crowded audiences, and was treated like a prince by them, but owing to declining health, I had to leave the city of Glasgow. Since this Book of Poems perhaps will be my last effort.

I earnestly hope the inhabitants of the beautiful city
    of Dundee
Will appreciate this little volume got up by me,
And when they read its pages, I hope it will fill their
    hearts with delight,
While seated around the fireside on a cold winter's
    night;
And some of them, no doubt, will let a silent tear fall
In dear remembrance of
            WILLIAM McGONAGALL.

TRIBUTE FROM THREE STUDENTS
AT GLASGOW UNIVERSITY

The University,
Glasgow, February 1891.

To WILLIAM M'GONAGALL,
Poet and Tragedian,
City of Dundee.

Dear Sir,—We, the undersigned, beg to send you herewith an Ode we have composed in your honour. We have had the extreme pleasure of reading your "Poetic Gems," and have embodied our sentiments in the poem referred to. We do not hope to receive a very favourable criticism upon our small effort, but as young men desirous to imitate the master of poetic art we have discovered in you, we trust you will be as lenient as possible with your enthusiastic disciples. We do not wish to rival your splendid achievements, as that would be as presumptuous as it would be futile, but if we can, afar off, emulate the performances of the poet of Dundee, or in a remote way catch any of his inspiration, our reward will be truly great. We beg, therefore, that you will write us, and inform us what you think of our poem. You might also reply, as far as you are able, to the following questions :—

I.   What grammar would you recommend as a preliminary study to the writing of poetry?

II. Is a College education an aid to write poetry, and what University would you recommend?

III. Is the most intellectual benefit to be derived from a study of the M'Gonagallian or Shakespearian school of poetry?

26

IV. Does your own success in the realms of poetry enable you to estimate what special capacity any of us may have for lyric poetry or the drama?

V. Would you recommend any of us to try our chance at the histrionic art; and if not, why not? Is Macbeth or Richard III. the best character to take up?

VI. Would you recommend us to write direct to the Queen as a patron of poetry; or should we go to Balmoral to see her there?

VII. What chances do you consider we have in knocking out Tennyson as Poet Laureate?

VIII. If we should resolve upon going to Balmoral, which route would you recommend? Also name any "models" that may be known to you in that direction; stating landlady's name, and if married or single.

We are, your admiring followers,

HENRY JOHN MACDONALD.
A. F. CAMPBELL.
S. DONALD STEWART.

ODE TO WILLIAM M'GONAGALL

POET AND TRAGEDIAN, DUNDEE

Among the poets of the present day
There is no one on earth who can possibly be able for to
gainsay
But that William M'Gonagall, poet and tragedian,
Is truly the greatest poet that was ever found above or
below the meridian.

'Twas in year '91, in the first month of spring,
On a very cold night, and the frost in full swing,
I met my friend Mactavish walking along the street,
And he gave me your "Poetic Gems" for them to read as
   a treat.

I took them home, and read them, and exclaimed,
Eureka! Eureka! M'Gonagall I proclaim
To have the deepest insight into human nature of any man
   I know,
As the reading of his "Gems" doth most emphatically show.

He reaches with poetic power the higher flights of song,
And like the eagle near the clouds, he soars serene and
   strong;
No common fowl is he, to roost on fence or crow about a
   barn,
He warbles sweet his wood-notes wild, and tell no common
   "yarn."

A better poet was never seen in the city of Dundee at any
   time,
And never again shall be, as far as I can see in the mean-
   time:
His poem on the Tay Bridge is most beautiful to be read,
As I found by reading it one cold night before I went
   to bed.

Also his poem about the Emperor of Germany's funeral is
   the work of a master-mind,
And rivals in merit the greatest plays that the "Bard of
   Avon" left behind,
And it will be read when Milton's "Paradise Lost" is totally
   forgotten,
And all other poetic gems save those of William M'Gona-
   gall are rotten.

But not till then will the world ever come to see
The wealth and beauty of the "Poetic Gems" of M'Gona-
   gall, poet and tragedian, of Dundee;

And though his book can now be bought at the modest
  price of a shilling,
You can never get anywhere, at any price, a product quite
  so thrilling.

At the beginning of the volume is to be seen the classic
  head
Of the greatest tragedian that ever the boards did tread,
For to act the Thane of Fife, or discourse with spirits from
  beneath,
And cry in tones of thunder : "Command ! they stand upon
the heath."

Also his ode on the death of George Gilfillan
Shows that he was a true gentleman and no villain;
His poem on the funeral of the illustrious Prince Leopold
Would almost make any one weep for to behold.

Any one who would read his lines on Queen Victoria
Would never again be troubled with melancholia,
Because she had been a good Queen, and by no means bad,
Which, if she were, would indeed be sad.

And though she did not receive M'Gonagall at her castle
  of Balmoral
The wreath that binds the poet's brow should be something
  more than floral,—
A wreath that will flourish evergreen in all the coming
  time,
When the name of the great M'Gonagall shall be known
  from clime to clime.

They will one day yet rear him monuments of brass, and
  weep upon his grave,
Though when he was living they would hardly give him
  the price of a shave;
But his peerless, priceless "Poetic Gems" will settle once
  for all
The claim to immortality of William M'Gonagall.

THE BATTLE OF TEL-EL-KEBIR

Ye sons of Great Britain, come join with me,
And sing in praise of Sir Garnet Wolseley;
Sound drums and trumpets cheerfully,
For he has acted most heroically.

Therefore loudly his praises sing
Until the hills their echoes back doth ring;
For he is a noble hero bold,
And an honour to his Queen and country, be it told.

He has gained for himself fame and renown,
Which to posterity will be handed down;
Because he has defeated Arabi by land and by sea,
And from the battle of Tel-el-Kebir he made him flee.

With an army about fourteen thousand strong,
Through Egypt he did fearlessly march along,
With the gallant and brave Highland brigade,
To whom honour is due, be it said.

Arabi's army was about seventy thousand in all,
And, virtually speaking, it wasn't very small;
But if they had been as numerous again,
The Irish and Highland brigades would have beaten them,
    it is plain.

'Twas on the 13th day of September, in the year of 1882,
Which Arabi and his rebel horde long will rue;
Because Sir Garnet Wolseley and his brave little band
Fought and conquered them on Kebir land.

He marched upon the enemy with his gallant band
O'er the wild and lonely desert sand,
And attacked them before daylight,
And in twenty minutes he put them to flight.

The first shock of the attack was borne by the Second
    Brigade,
Who behaved most manfully, it is said,
Under the command of brave General Grahame,
And have gained a lasting honour to their name.

But Major Hart and the 18th Royal Irish, conjoint,
Carried the trenches at the bayonet's point;
Then the Marines chased them about four miles away,
At the charge of the bayonet, without dismay!

General Sir Archibald Alison led on the Highland Brigade,
Who never were the least afraid.
And such has been the case in this Egyptian war,
For at the charge of the bayonet they ran them from afar!

With their bagpipes playing, and one ringing cheer,
And the 42nd soon did the trenches clear;
Then hand to hand they did engage,
And fought like tigers in a cage.

Oh! it must have been a glorious sight
To see Sir Garnet Wolseley in the thickest of the fight!
In the midst of shot and shell, and the cannon's roar,
Whilst the dead and the dying lay weltering in their gore.

Then the Egyptians were forced to yield,
And the British were left masters of the field;
Then Arabi he did fret and frown
To see his army thus cut down.

Then Arabi the rebel took to flight,
And spurred his Arab steed with all his might;
With his heart full of despair and woe,
And never halted till he reached Cairo.

Now since the Egyptian war is at an end,
Let us thank God! Who did send
Sir Garnet Wolseley to crush and kill
Arabi and his rebel army at Kebir hill.

THE FAMOUS TAY WHALE

'Twas in the month of December, and in the year 1883,
That a monster whale came to Dundee,
Resolved for a few days to sport and play,
And devour the small fishes in the silvery Tay.

So the monster whale did sport and play
Among the innocent little fishes in the beautiful Tay,
Until he was seen by some men one day,
And they resolved to catch them without delay.

When it came to be known a whale was seen in the Tay,
Some men began to talk and say,
We must try and catch this monster of a whale,
So come on, brave boys, and never say fail.

Then the people together in crowds did run,
Resolved to capture the whale and to have some fun!
So small boats were launched on the silvery Tay,
While the monster of the deep did sport and play.

Oh! it was a most fearful and beautiful sight,
To see it lashing the water with its tail all its might,
And making the water ascend like a shower of hail,
With one lash of its ugly and mighty tail.

Then the water did descend on the men in the boats,
Which wet their trousers and also their coats;
But it only made them the more determined to catch the
    whale,
But the whale shook at them his tail.

Then the whale began to puff and to blow,
While the men and the boats after him did go,
Armed well with harpoons for the fray,
Which they fired at him without dismay.

And they laughed and grinned just like wild baboons,
While they fired at him their sharp harpoons:
But when struck with the harpoons he dived below,
Which filled his pursuers' hearts with woe:

Because they guessed they had lost a prize,
Which caused the tears to well up in their eyes;
And in that their anticipations were only right,
Because he sped on to Stonehaven with all his might:

And was first seen by the crew of a Gourdon fishing boat,
Which they thought was a big coble upturned afloat;
But when they drew near they saw it was a whale,
So they resolved to tow it ashore without fail.

So they got a rope from each boat tied round his tail,
And landed their burden at Stonehaven without fail;
And when the people saw it their voices they did raise,
Declaring that the brave fishermen deserved great praise.

And my opinion is that God sent the whale in time of
     need,
No matter what other people may think or what is their
     creed;
I know fishermen in general are often very poor,
And God in His goodness sent it to drive poverty from their
     door.

So Mr John Wood has bought it for two hundred and
     twenty-six pound,
And has brought it to Dundee all safe and all sound;
Which measures 40 feet in length from the snout to the tail,
So I advise the people near and far to see it without fail.

Then hurrah! for the mighty monster whale,
Which has got 17 feet 4 inches from tip to tip of a tail!
Which can be seen for a sixpence or a shilling,
That is to say, if the people all are willing.

THE RAILWAY BRIDGE OF THE SILVERY TAY

BEAUTIFUL Railway Bridge of the Silvery Tay!
With your numerous arches and pillars in so grand array,
And your central girders, which seem to the eye
To be almost towering to the sky.
The greatest wonder of the day,
And a great beautification to the River Tay,
Most beautiful to be seen,
Near by Dundee and the Magdalen Green.

Beautiful Railway Bridge of the Silvery Tay!
That has caused the Emperor of Brazil to leave
His home far away, *incognito* in his dress,
And view thee ere he passed along *en route* to Inverness.

Beautiful Railway Bridge of the Silvery Tay!
The longest of the present day
That has ever crossed o'er a tidal river stream,
Most gigantic to be seen,
Near by Dundee and the Magdalen Green.

Beautiful Railway Bridge of the Silvery Tay!
Which will cause great rejoicing on the opening day,
And hundreds of people will come from far away,
Also the Queen, most gorgeous to be seen,
Near by Dundee and the Magdalen Green.

Beautiful Railway Bridge of the Silvery Tay!
And prosperity to Provost Cox, who has given
Thirty thousand pounds and upwards away
In helping to erect the Bridge of the Tay,
Near by Dundee and the Magdalen Green.
Most handsome to be seen,

Beautiful Railway Bridge of the Silvery Tay!
I hope that God will protect all passengers
By night and by day,
And that no accident will befall them while crossing
The Bridge of the Silvery Tay,
For that would be most awful to be seen
Near by Dundee and the Magdalen Green.

Beautiful Railway Bridge of the Silvery Tay!
And prosperity to Messrs Bouche and Grothe,
The famous engineers of the present day,
Who have succeeded in erecting the Railway
Bridge of the Silvery Tay,
Which stands unequalled to be seen
Near by Dundee and the Magdalen Green.

THE NEWPORT RAILWAY

Success to the Newport Railway,
Along the braes of the Silvery Tay,
And to Dundee straightway,
Across the Railway Bridge o' the Silvery Tay,
Which was opened on the 12th of May,
In the year of our Lord 1879,
Which will clear all expenses in a very short time
Because the thrifty housewives of Newport
To Dundee will often resort,
Which will be to them profit and sport,
By bringing cheap tea, bread, and jam,
And also some of Lipton's ham,
Which will make their hearts feel light and gay,
And cause them to bless the opening day
Of the Newport Railway.

The train is most beautiful to be seen,
With its long, white curling cloud of steam,
As the train passes on her way
Along the bonnie braes o' the Silvery Tay.

And if the people of Dundee
Should feel inclined to have a spree,
I am sure 'twill fill their hearts with glee
By crossing o'er to Newport,
And there they can have excellent sport,
By viewing the scenery beautiful and gay,
During the livelong summer day.

And then they can return at night
With spirits light and gay,
By the Newport Railway,
By night or by day,
Across the Railway Bridge o' the Silvery Tay.

Success to the undertakers of the Newport Railway,
Hoping the Lord will their labours repay,
And prove a blessing to the people
For many a long day
Who live near by Newport,
On the bonnie braes o' the Silvery Tay.

THE TAY BRIDGE DISASTER

BEAUTIFUL Railway Bridge of the Silv'ry Tay!
Alas! I am very sorry to say
That ninety lives have been taken away
On the last Sabbath day of 1879,
Which will be remember'd for a very long time.

'Twas about seven o'clock at night,
And the wind it blew with all its might,
And the rain came pouring down,
And the dark clouds seem'd to frown,
And the Demon of the air seem'd to say—
"I'll blow down the Bridge of Tay."

When the train left Edinburgh
The passengers' hearts were light and felt no sorrow,
But Boreas blew a terrific gale,
Which made their hearts for to quail,
And many of the passengers with fear did say—
"I hope God will send us safe across the Bridge of Tay."

But when the train came near to Wormit Bay,
Boreas he did long and angry bray,
And shook the central girders of the Bridge of Tay
On the last Sabbath day of 1879,
Which will be remember'd for a very long time.

So the train sped on with all its might,
And Bonnie Dundee soon hove in sight,
And the passengers' hearts felt light,
Thinking they would enjoy themselves on the New Year,
With their friends at home they lov'd most dear,
And wish them all a Happy New Year.

So the train mov'd slowly along the Bridge of Tay,
Until it was about midway,
Then the central girders with a crash gave way,
And down went the train and passengers into the Tay!
The Storm Fiend did loudly bray,
Because ninety lives had been taken away,
On the last Sabbath day of 1879,
Which will be remember'd for a very long time.

As soon as the catastrophe came to be known
The alarm from mouth to mouth was blown,
And the cry rang out all o'er the town,
Good Heavens! the Tay Bridge is blown down,
And a passenger train from Edinburgh,
Which fill'd all the people's hearts with sorrow,
And made them for to turn pale,
Because none of the passengers were sav'd to tell the tale
How the disaster happen'd on the last Sabbath day of 1879
Which will be remember'd for a very long time.

It must have been an awful sight,
To witness in the dusky moonlight,
While the Storm Fiend did laugh, and angry did bray,
Along the Railway Bridge of the Silv'ry Tay.
Oh ! ill-fated Bridge of the Silv'ry Tay,
I must now conclude my lay
By telling the world fearlessly without the least dismay,
That your central girders would not have given way,
At least many sensible men do say,
Had they been supported on each side with buttresses,
At least many sensible men confesses,
For the stronger we our houses do build,
The less chance we have of being killed.

AN ADDRESS TO THE NEW TAY BRIDGE

BEAUTIFUL new railway bridge of the Silvery Tay,
With your strong brick piers and buttresses in so grand
    array,
And your thirteen central girders, which seem to my eye
Strong enough all windy storms to defy.
And as I gaze upon thee my heart feels gay,
Because thou are the greatest railway bridge of the present
    day,
And can be seen for miles away
From north, south, east, or west of the Tay
On a beautiful and clear sunshiny day,
And ought to make the hearts of the "Mars" boys feel gay,
Because thine equal nowhere can be seen,
Only near by Dundee and the bonnie Magdalen Green.

Beautiful new railway bridge of the Silvery Tay,
With thy beautiful side-screens along your railway,
Which will be a great protection on a windy day,
So as the railway carriages won't be blown away,
And ought to cheer the hearts of the passengers night and
    day

As they are conveyed along thy beautiful railway,
And towering above the silvery Tay,
Spanning the beautiful river shore to shore
Upwards of two miles or more,
Which is most wonderful to be seen
Near by Dundee and the bonnie Magdalen Green.

Thy structure to my eye seems strong and grand,
And the workmanship most skilfully planned;
And I hope the designers, Messrs Barlow & Arrol, will
    prosper for many a day
For erecting thee across the beautiful Tay.
And I think nobody need have the least dismay
To cross o'er thee by night or by day,
Because thy strength is visible to be seen
Near by Dundee and the bonnie Magdalen Green.

Beautiful new railway bridge of the Silvery Tay,
I wish you success for many a year and a day,
And I hope thousands of people will come from far away,
Both high and low without delay,
From the north, south, east, and the west,
Because as a railway bridge thou are the best;
Thou standest unequalled to be seen
Near by Dundee and the bonnie Magdalen Green.

And for beauty thou art most lovely to be seen
As the train crosses o'er thee with her cloud of steam;
And you look well, painted the colour of marone,
And to find thy equal there is none,
Which, without fear of contradiction, I venture to say,
Because you are the longest bridge of the present day
That now crosses o'er a tidal river stream,
And the most handsome to be seen
Near by Dundee and the bonnie Magdalen Green.

The New Yorkers boast about their Brooklyn Bridge,
But in comparison to thee it seems like a midge,
Because thou spannest the silvery Tay
A mile or more longer I venture to say;

Besides the railway carriages are pulled across by a rope,
Therefore Brooklyn Bridge cannot with thee cope;
And as you have been opened on the 20th day of June,
I hope Her Majesty Queen Victoria will visit thee very
    soon.
Because thou are worthy of a visit from Duke, Lord, or
    Queen,
And strong and securely built, which is most worthy to be
    seen
Near by Dundee and the bonnie Magdalen Green.

THE BATTLE OF EL-TEB

Ye sons of Great Britain, I think no shame
To write in praise of brave General Graham!
Whose name will be handed down to posterity without any
    stigma,
Because, at the battle of El-Teb, he defeated Osman Digna.

With an army about five thousand strong,
To El-Teb, in the year 1884, he marched along,
And bivouacked there for the night;
While around their fires they only thought of the coming
    fight.

They kept up their fires all the long night,
Which made the encampment appear weird-like to the
    sight;
While the men were completely soaked with the rain,
But the brave heroes disdained to complain.

The brave heroes were glad when daylight did appear,
And when the reveille was sounded, they gave a hearty
    cheer
And their fires were piled up higher again,
Then they tried to dry their clothes that were soaked with
    the rain.

Then breakfast was taken about eight o'clock,
And when over, each man stood in the ranks as firm as a
    rock,
And every man seemed to be on his guard—
All silent and ready to move forward.

The first movement was a short one from where they lay—
Then they began to advance towards El-Teb without
    dismay,
And showed that all was in order for the fray,
While every man's heart seemed to feel light and gay.

The enemy's position could be seen in the distance far away,
But the brave heroes marched on without delay—
Whilst the enemy's banners floated in the air,
And dark swarms of men were scattered near by there.

Their force was a large one—its front extended over a mile,
And all along the line their guns were all in file;
But, as the British advanced, they disappeared,
While our brave kilty lads loudly cheered.

Thus slowly and cautiously brave General Graham pro-
    ceeded,
And to save his men from slaughter, great caution was
    needed,
Because Osman Digna's force was about ten thousand
    strong,
But he said, Come on, my brave lads, we'll conquer them
    ere long!

It was about ten o'clock when they came near the enemy's
    lines,
And on the morning air could be heard the cheerful chimes
Coming from the pipes of the gallant Black Watch,
Which every ear in the British force was eager to catch.

Then they passed by the enemy about mid-day,
While every Arab seemed to have his gun ready for the
    fray;
When a bullet strikes down General Baker by the way,
But he is soon in the saddle again without delay.

And ready for any service that he could perform;
Whilst the bullets fell around them in a perfect storm
That they had to lie down, but not through fear,
Because the enemy was about 800 yards on their left rear.

Then General Graham addressed his men,
And said, If they won't attack us, we must attack them,
So start to your feet my lads, and never fear,
And strike up your bagpipes, and give a loud cheer.

So they leapt to their feet, and gave a loud cheer,
While the Arabs swept down upon them without the least
   fear,
And put aside their rifles, and grasped their spears;
Whilst the British bullets in front of them the earth uptears.

Then the British charged them with their cold steel,
Which made the Arabs backwards for to reel;
But they dashed forward again on their ranks without
   dismay,
But before the terrible fire of their musketry they were
   swept away.

Oh! God of Heaven! it was a terrible sight
To see, and hear the Arabs shouting with all their might
A fearful oath when they got an inch of cold steel,
Which forced them backwards again, and made them reel.

By two o'clock they were fairly beat,
And Osman Digna, the false prophet, was forced to retreat
After three hours of an incessant fight;
But Heaven, 'tis said, defends the right.

And I think he ought to be ashamed of himself;
For I consider he has acted the part of a silly elf,
By thinking to conquer the armies of the Lord
With his foolish and benighted rebel horde.

AN AUTUMN REVERIE

Alas ! beautiful Summer now hath fled,
And the face of Nature doth seem dead,
And the leaves are withered, and falling off the trees,
By the nipping and chilling autumnal breeze.

The pleasures of the little birds are all fled,
And with the cold many of them will be found dead,
Because the leaves of the trees are scattered in the blast,
And makes the feathered creatures seem downcast.

Because there are no leaves on the trees to shield them from
     the storm
On a windy, and rainy, cloudy morn;
Which makes their little hearts throb with pain,
By the chilling blast and the pitiless rain.

But still they are more contented than the children of God,
As long as they can pick up a worm from the sod,
Or anything they can get to eat,
Just, for instance, a stale crust of bread or a grain of wheat.

Oh ! think of the little birds in the time of snow,
Also of the little street waifs, that are driven to and fro,
And trembling in the cold blast, and chilled to the bone,
For the want of food and clothing, and a warm home.

Besides think of the sorrows of the wandering poor,
That are wandering in the cold blast from door to door;
And begging, for Heaven's sake, a crust of bread,
And alas ! not knowing where to lay their head.

While the rich are well fed and covered from the cold,
While the poor are starving, both young and old;
Alas! it is the case in this boasted Christian land,
Whereas the rich are told to be kind to the poor, is God's
    command.

Oh! think of the working man when he's no work to do,
Who's got a wife and family, perhaps four or two,
And the father searching for work, and no work can be had,
The thought, I'm sure, 'tis enough to drive the poor man
    mad.

Because for his wife and family he must feel,
And perhaps the thought thereof will cause him to steal
Bread for his family, that are starving at home,
Whilst the thought thereof makes him sigh heavily and
    groan.

Alas! the pangs of hunger are very hard to thole,
And few people can their temper control,
Or become reconciled to their fate,
Especially when they cannot find anything to eat.

Oh! think of the struggles of the poor to make a living,
Because the rich unto them seldom are giving;
Whereas they are told he that giveth to the poor lendeth
    unto the Lord,
But alas! they rather incline their money to hoard.

Then there's the little news-vendors in the street,
Running about perhaps with bare feet;
And if the rich chance to see such creatures in the street,
In general they make a sudden retreat.

THE WRECK OF THE STEAMER "LONDON"

WHILE ON HER WAY TO AUSTRALIA

'Twas in the year of 1866, and on a very beautiful day,
That eighty-two passengers, with spirits light and gay,
Left Gravesend harbour, and sailed gaily away
On board the steamship "London,"
Bound for the city of Melbourne,
Which unfortunately was her last run,
Because she was wrecked on the stormy main,
Which has caused many a heart to throb with pain,
Because they will ne'er look upon their lost ones again.

'Twas on the 11th of January they anchored at the Nore;
The weather was charming—the like was seldom seen
      before,
Especially the next morning as they came in sight
Of the charming and beautiful Isle of Wight,
But the wind it blew a terrific gale towards night,
Which caused the passengers' hearts to shake with fright,
And caused many of them to sigh and mourn,
And whisper to themselves, We will ne'er see Melbourne.

Among the passengers was Gustavus V. Brooke,
Who was to be seen walking on the poop,
Also clergymen, and bankers, and magistrates also,
All chatting merrily together in the cabin below;
And also wealthy families returning to their dear native
      land,
And accomplished young ladies, most lovely and grand,
All in the beauty and bloom of their pride,
And some with their husbands sitting close by their side.

45

'Twas all of a sudden the storm did arise,
Which took the captain and passengers all by surprise,
Because they had just sat down to their tea,
When the ship began to roll with the heaving of the sea,
And shipped a deal of water, which came down upon their
    heads,
Which wet their clothes and also their beds;
And caused a fearful scene of consternation,
And among the ladies great tribulation,
And made them cry out, Lord, save us from being drowned,
And for a few minutes the silence was profound.

Then the passengers began to run to and fro,
With buckets to bale out the water between decks below,
And Gustavus Brooke quickly leapt from his bed
In his Garibaldi jacket and drawers, without fear or dread,
And rushed to the pump, and wrought with might and
    main;
But alas! all their struggling was in vain,
For the water fast did on them gain;
But he enacted a tragic part until the last,
And sank exhausted when all succour was past;
When the big billows did lash her o'er,
And the Storm-fiend did laugh and roar.

Oh, Heaven! it must have really been
A most harrowing and pitiful scene
To hear mothers and their children loudly screaming,
And to see the tears adown their pale faces streaming,
And to see a clergyman engaged in prayer,
Imploring God their lives to spare, ...
Whilst the cries of the women and children did rend the air.

Then the captain cried, Lower down the small boats,
And see if either of them sinks or floats;
Then the small boats were launched on the stormy wave,
And each one tried had his life to save
From a merciless watery grave. . . . . .

A beautiful young lady did madly cry and rave,
"Five hundred sovereigns, my life to save!"
But she was by the sailors plainly told
For to keep her filthy gold, ...
Because they were afraid to overload the boat,
Therefore she might either sink or float,
Then she cast her eyes to Heaven, and cried, Lord, save me,
Then went down with the ship to the bottom of the sea,
Along with Gustavus Brooke, who was wont to fill our
hearts with glee
While performing Shakespearian tragedy.

And out of eighty-two passengers only twenty were saved,
And that twenty survivors most heroically behaved.
For three stormy days and stormy nights they were tossed
    to and fro
On the raging billows, with their hearts full of woe,
Alas! poor souls, not knowing where to go,
Until at last they all agreed to steer for the south,
And they chanced to meet an Italian barque bound for
    Falmouth,
And they were all rescued from a watery grave,
And they thanked God and Captain Cavassa, who did their
    lives save.

ATTEMPTED ASSASSINATION
OF THE QUEEN

God prosper long our noble Queen,
    And long may she reign!
Maclean he tried to shoot her,
    But it was all in vain.

For God He turned the ball aside
    Maclean aimed at her head;
And he felt very angry
    Because he didn't shoot her dead.

There's a divinity that hedgeth a king,
    And so it does seem,
And my opinion is, it has hedged
    Our most gracious Queen.

Maclean must be a madman,
    Which is obvious to be seen,
Or else he wouldn't have tried to shoot
    Our most beloved Queen.

Victoria is a good Queen,
    Which all her subjects know,
And for that God has protected her
    From all her deadly foes.

She is noble and generous,
    Her subjects must confess;
There hasn't been her equal
    Since the days of good Queen Bess.

Long may she be spared to roam
    Among the bonnie Highland floral,
And spend many a happy day
    In the palace of Balmoral.

Because she is very kind
    To the old women there,
And allows them bread, tea, and sugar,
    And each one to get a share.

And when they know of her coming,
    Their hearts feel overjoy'd,
Because, in general, she finds work
    For men that's unemployed.

And she also gives the gipsies money
    While at Balmoral, I've been told,
And, mind ye, seldom silver,
    But very often gold.

I hope God will protect her
  By night and by day,
At home and abroad
  When she's far away.

May he be as a hedge around her,
  As He's been all along,
And let her live and die in peace
  Is the end of my song.

THE MOON

BEAUTIFUL Moon, with thy silvery light,
Thou seemest most charming to my sight;
As I gaze upon thee in the sky so high,
A tear of joy does moisten mine eye.

Beautiful Moon, with thy silvery light,
Thou cheerest the Esquimau in the night;
For thou lettest him see to harpoon the fish
And with them he makes a dainty dish.

Beautiful Moon, with thy silvery light,
Thou cheerest the fox in the night,
And lettest him see to steal the grey goose away
Out of the farm-yard from a stack of hay.

Beautiful Moon, with thy silvery light,
Thou cheerest the farmer in the night,
And makest his heart beat high with delight
As he views his crops by the light in the night.

Beautiful Moon, with thy silvery light,
Thou cheerest the eagle in the night,
And lettest him see to devour his prey
And carry it to his nest away.

Beautiful Moon, with thy silvery light,
Thou cheerest the mariner in the night
As he paces the decks alone,
Thinking of his dear friends at home.

Beautiful Moon, with thy silvery light,
Thou cheerest the weary traveller in the night;
For thou lightest up the wayside around
To him when he is homeward bound.

Beautiful Moon, with thy silvery light,
Thou cheerest the lovers in the night
As they walk through the shady groves alone,
Making love to each other before they go home.

Beautiful Moon, with thy silvery light,
Thou cheerest the poacher in the night;
For thou lettest him see to set his snares
To catch the rabbits and the hares.

THE BEAUTIFUL SUN

BEAUTIFUL SUN! with thy golden rays,
To God, the wise Creator, be all praise;
For thou nourisheth all the creation,
Wherever there is to be found to be animation.

Without thy heat we could not live,
Then praise to God we ought to give;
For thou makest the fruits and provisions to grow,
To nourish all creatures on earth below.

Thou makest the hearts of the old feel glad,
Likewise the young child and the lad,
And the face of Nature to look green and gay,
And the little children to sport and play.

Thou also givest light unto the Moon,
Which certainly is a very great boon
To all God's creatures here below,
Throughout the world where'er they go.

How beautiful thou look'st on a summer morn,
When thou sheddest thy effulgence among the yellow corn,
Also upon lake, and river, and the mountain tops,
Whilst thou leavest behind the most lovely dewdrops!

How beautiful thou seem'st in the firmament above,
As I gaze upon thee, my heart fills with love
To God, the great Creator, Who has placed thee there,
Who watches all His creatures with an eye of care!

Thou makest the birds to sing on the tree,
Also by meadow, mountain, and lea;
And the lark high poised up in air,
Carolling its little song with its heart free from care.

Thou makest the heart of the shepherd feel gay
As he watches the little lambkins at their innocent play;
While he tends them on the hillside all day,
Taking care that none of them shall go astray.

Thou cheerest the weary traveller while on his way
During the livelong summer day,
As he admires the beautiful scenery while passing along,
And singing to himself a stave of a song.

Thou cheerest the tourist while amongst the Highland hills,
As he views their beautiful sparkling rills
Glittering like diamonds by thy golden rays
While the hills seem to offer up to God their praise.

While the bee from flower to flower does roam
To gather honey, and carry it home;
While it hums its little song in the beautiful sunshine,
And seemingly to thank the Creator divine—

For the honey it hath gathered during the day,
In the merry month of May,
When the flowers are in full bloom,
Also the sweet honeysuckle and the broom.

How beautiful thy appearance while setting in the west,
Whilst encircled with red and azure, 'tis then thou look'st
    best!
Then let us all thank God for thy golden light
In our prayers every morning and night!

GRACE DARLING

OR

THE WRECK OF THE "FORFARSHIRE"

As the night was beginning to close in one rough September
    day
In the year of 1838, a steamer passed through the Fairway
Between the Farne Islands and the coast, on her passage
    northwards;
But the wind was against her, and the steamer laboured
    hard.

There she laboured in the heavy sea against both wind and
    tide,
While a dense fog enveloped her on every side;
And the mighty billows made her timbers creak,
Until at last, unfortunately, she sprung a leak.

Then all hands rushed to the pumps, and wrought with
    might and main.
But the water, alas! alarmingly on them did gain;
And the thick sleet was driving across the raging sea,
While the wind it burst upon them in all its fury.

And the fearful gale and the murky aspect of the sky
Caused the passengers on board to lament and sigh
As the sleet drove thick, furious, and fast.
And as the waves surged mountains high, they stood aghast.

And the screaming of the sea-birds fortold a gathering
    storm,
And the passengers, poor souls, looked pale and forlorn,
And on every countenance was depicted woe
As the "Forfarshire" steamer was pitched to and fro.

And the engine-fires with the water were washed out;
Then, as the tide set strongly in, it wheeled the vessel about,
And the ill-fated steamer drifted helplessly along;
But the fog cleared up a little as the night wore on.

Then the terror-stricken crew saw the breakers ahead,
And all thought of being saved from them fled;
And the Farne lights were shining hazily through the
    gloom,
While in the fore-cabin a woman lay with two children in
    a swoon.

Before the morning broke, the "Forfarshire" struck upon
    a rock,
And was dashed to pieces by a tempestuous shock,
Which raised her for a moment, and dashed her down
    again,
Then the ill-starred vessel was swallowed up in the briny
    main.

Before the vessel broke up, some nine or ten of the crew
    intent
To save their lives, or perish in the attempt,
Lowered one of the boats while exhausted and forlorn,
And, poor souls, were soon lost sight of in the storm.

Around the windlass on the forecastle some dozen poor
    wretches clung,
As the merciless sea broke o'er them every moment;
And with despair and grief their weakly hearts were rung
But God in His mercy to them Grace Darling sent.

By the first streak of dawn she early up had been,
And happened to look out upon the stormy scene,
And she descried the wreck through the morning gloom;
But she resolved to rescue them from such a perilous doom.

Then she cried, Oh! father dear, come here and see the
    wreck,
See, here take the telescope, and you can inspect;
Oh! father, try and save them, and heaven will you bless;
But, my darling, no help can reach them in such a storm
    as this.

Oh! my kind father, you will surely try and save
These poor souls from a cold and watery grave;
Oh! I cannot sit to see them perish before mine eyes,
And, for the love of heaven, do not my pleading despise!

Then old Darling yielded, and launched the little boat,
And high on the big waves the boat did float;
Then Grace and her father took each an oar in hand,
And to see Grace Darling rowing the picture was grand.

And as the little boat to the sufferers drew near,
Poor souls, they tried to raise a cheer;
But as they gazed upon the heroic Grace,
The big tears trickled down each sufferer's face.

And nine persons were rescued almost dead with the cold
By modest and lovely Grace Darling, that heroine bold;
The survivors were taken to the light-house, and remained
    there two days,
And every one of them was loud in Grace Darling's praise.

Grace Darling was a comely lass, with long, fair floating
  hair,
With soft blue eyes, and shy, and modesty rare.
And her countenance was full of sense and genuine
With a noble heart, and ready to help suffering creatures
  in distress.

But, alas! three years after her famous exploit,
Which, to the end of time, will never be forgot,
Consumption, that fell destroyer, carried her away
To heaven, I hope, to be an angel for ever and aye.

Before she died, scores of suitors in marriage sought her
  hand;
But no, she'd rather live in Longstone light-house on Farne
  island,
And there she lived and died with her father and mother,
And for her equal in true heroism we cannot find another.

THE BATTLE OF BANNOCKBURN

Sir Robert the Bruce at Bannockburn
Beat the English in every wheel and turn,
And made them fly in great dismay
From off the field without delay.

The English were a hundred thousand strong,
And King Edward passed through the Lowlands all along,
Determined to conquer Scotland, it was his desire,
And then to restore it to his own empire.

King Edward brought numerous waggons in his train,
Expecting that most of the Scottish army would be slain,
Hoping to make the rest prisoners, and carry them away
In waggon-loads to London without delay.

The Scottish army did not amount to more than thirty
    thousand strong;
But Bruce had confidence he'd conquer his foes ere long;
So, to protect his little army, he thought it was right
To have deep-dug pits made in the night;

And caused them to be overlaid with turf and brushwood
Expecting the plan would prove effectual where his little
    army stood,
Waiting patiently for the break of day,
All willing to join in the deadly fray.

Bruce stationed himself at the head of the reserve,
Determined to conquer, but never to swerve,
And by his side were brave Kirkpatrick and true De
    Longueville,
Both trusty warriors, firm and bold, who would never him
    beguile.

By daybreak the whole of the English army came in view,
Consisting of archers and horsemen, bold and true;
The main body was led on by King Edward himself,
An avaricious man, and fond of pelf.

The Abbot of Inchaffray celebrated mass,
And all along the Scottish lines he did pass,
With the crucifix in his hand, a most beautiful sight to see,
Exhorting them to trust in God, and He would set them
    free.

Then the Scottish army knelt down on the field,
And King Edward he thought they were going to yield,
And he felt o'erjoyed, and cried to Earl Percy,
"See ! See ! the Scots are crying for mercy."

But Percy said, "Your Majesty need not make such a fuss,
They are crying for mercy from God, not from us;
For, depend upon it, they will fight to a man, and find
    their graves
Rather than yield to become your slaves."

Then King Edward ordered his horsemen to charge,
Thirty thousand in number, it was very large;
They thought to o'erwhelm them ere they could rise from
    their knees,
But they met a different destiny, which did them displease;
For the horsemen fell in the spik'd pits in the way,
And, with broken ranks and confusion, they all fled away,
But few of them escap'd death from the spik'd pits,
For the Scots with their swords hack'd them to bits;
De Valence was overthrown and carried off the field
Then King Edward he thought it was time to yield.

And he uttered a fearful cry
To his gay archers near by,
Ho! archers! draw your arrows to the head,
And make sure to kill them dead;
Forward, without dread, and make them fly
Saint George for England, be our cry!

Then the arrows from their bows swiftly did go,
And fell amongst them as thick as the flakes of snow;
Then Bruce he drew his trusty blade,
And in heroic language said,
Forward, my heroes, bold and true!
And break the archers' ranks through and through!
And charge them boldly with your swords in hand,
And chase these vultures from off our land,
And make King Edward mourn
The day he came to Bannockburn.

See proud Edward on his milk-white steed,
One of England's finest breed,
Coming here in grand array,
With horsemen bold and archers gay,
Thinking he will us dismay,
And sweep everything before him in his way;
But I swear by yon blessed sun
I'll make him and his army run
From off the field of Bannockburn.

By St. Andrew and our God most high,
We'll conquer these epicures or die !
And make them fly like chaff before the wind
Until they can no refuge find;
And beat them off the field without delay,
Like lions bold and heroes gay.
Upon them !—charge !—follow me,
For Scotland's rights and liberty !

Then the Scots charged them with sword in hand,
And made them fly from off their land;
And King Edward was amazed at the sight,
And he got wounded in the fight;
And he cried, Oh, heaven ! England's lost, and I'm undone,
Alas ! alas ! where shall I run?
Then he turned his horse, and rode on afar,
And never halted till he reached Dunbar.

Then Bruce he shouted, Victory !
We have gained our rights and liberty;
And thanks be to God above
That we have conquered King Edward this day,
A usurper that does not us love.

Then the Scots did shout and sing,
Long live Sir Robert Bruce our King !
That made King Edward mourn
The day he came to Bannockburn !

EDINBURGH

BEAUTIFUL city of Edinburgh !
Where the tourist can drown his sorrow
By viewing your monuments and statues fine
During the lovely summer-time.
I'm sure it will his spirits cheer
As Sir Walter Scott's monument he draws near,

That stands in East Princes Street
Amongst flowery gardens, fine and neat.
And Edinburgh castle is magnificent to be seen
With its beautiful walks and trees so green,
Which seem like a fairy dell;
And near by its rocky basement is St. Margaret's well,
Where the tourist can drink at when he feels dry,
And view the castle from beneath so very high,
Which seems almost towering to the sky.
Then as for Nelson's monument that stands on the Calton
    hill,
As the tourist gazes thereon, with wonder his heart does fill
As he thinks on Admiral Nelson who did the Frenchmen
    kill.
Then, as for Salisbury crags, they are most beautiful to be
    seen,
Especially in the month of June, when the grass is green;
There numerous mole-hills can be seen,
And the busy little creatures howking away,
Searching for worms amongst the clay;
And as the tourist's eye does wander to and fro
From the south side of Salisbury crags below,
His bosom with admiration feels all aglow
As he views the beautiful scenery in the valley below;
And if, with an observant eye, the little loch below he scans,
He can see the wild ducks swimming about and beautiful
    white swans.
Then, as for Arthur's seat, I'm sure it is a treat
Most worthy to be seen, with its rugged rocks and pastures
    green,
And the sheep browsing on its sides
To and fro, with slow-paced strides,
And the little lambkins at play
During the livelong summer-day.
Beautiful city of Edinburgh! the truth to express,
Your beauties are matchless I must confess,
And which no one dare gainsay
But that you are the grandest city in Scotland at the
    present day!

GLASGOW

BEAUTIFUL city of Glasgow, with your streets so neat and
    clean,
Your stately mansions, and beautiful Green!
Likewise your beautiful bridges across the river Clyde,
And on your bonnie banks I would like to reside.

Chorus—
    Then away to the West—to the beautiful West!
    To the fair city of Glasgow that I like the best,
    Where the river Clyde rolls on to the sea,
    And the lark and the blackbird whistle with glee.

'Tis beautiful to see the ships passing to and fro,
Laden with goods for the high and the low;
So let the beautiful city of Glasgow flourish,
And may the inhabitants always find food their bodies to
    nourish.

Chorus

The statue of the Prince of Orange is very grand,
Looking terror to the foe, with a truncheon in his hand,
And well mounted on a noble steed, which stands in the
    Trongate,
And holding up its foreleg, I'm sure it looks first-rate.

Chorus

Then there's the Duke of Wellington's statue in Royal
    Exchange Square—
It is a beautiful statue I without fear declare,
Besides inspiring and most magnificent to view,
Because he made the French fly at the battle of Waterloo.

Chorus

And as for the statue of Sir Walter Scott that stands in
George Square,
It is a handsome statue—few can with it compare,
And most elegant to be seen,
And close beside it stands the statue of Her Majesty the
Queen.

Chorus

Then there's the statue of Robert Burns in George Square,
And the treatment he received when living was very unfair;
Now, when he's dead, Scotland's sons for him do mourn,
But, alas! unto them he can never return.

Chorus

Then as for Kelvin Grove, it is most lovely to be seen
With its beautiful flowers and trees so green,
And a magnificent water-fountain spouting up very high,
Where the people can quench their thirst when they feel
dry.

Chorus

Beautiful city of Glasgow, I now conclude my muse,
And to write in praise of thee my pen does not refuse;
And, without fear of contradiction, I will venture to say
You are the second grandest city in Scotland at the present
day!

Chorus

GREENLAND'S ICY MOUNTAINS

Greenland's icy mountains are fascinating and grand,
And wondrously created by the Almighty's command;
And the works of the Almighty there's few can understand:
Who knows but it might be a part of Fairyland?

Because there are churches of ice, and houses glittering like
    glass,
And for scenic grandeur there's nothing can it surpass,
Besides there's monuments and spires, also ruins,
Which serve for a safe retreat from the wild bruins.

And there's icy crags and precipices, also beautiful water-
    falls,
And as the stranger gazes thereon, his heart it appals
With a mixture of wonder, fear, and delight,
Till at last he exclaims, Oh! what a wonderful sight!

The icy mountains they're higher than a brig's topmast,
And the stranger in amazement stands aghast
As he beholds the water flowing off the melted ice
Adown the mountain sides, that he cries out, Oh! how
    nice!

Such sights as these are truly magnificent to be seen,
Only that the mountain tops are white instead of green,
And rents and caverns in them, the same as on a rugged
    mountainside,
And suitable places, in my opinion, for mermaids to reside.

Sometimes these icy mountains suddenly topple o'er
With a wild and rumbling hollow-startling roar;
And new peaks and cliffs rise up out of the sea,
While great cataracts of uplifted brine pour down furiously.

And those that can witness such an awful sight
Can only gaze thereon in solemn silence and delight,
And the most Godfearless man that hath this region trod
Would be forced to recognise the power and majesty of
    God.

Oh ! how awful and grand it must be on a sunshiny day
To see one of these icy mountains in pieces give way !
While, crack after crack, it falls with a mighty crash
Flat upon the sea with a fearful splash.

When these icy mountains are falling, the report is like big
    guns,
And the glittering brilliancy of them causes mock-suns,
And around them there's connected a beautiful ring of
    light,
And as the stranger looks thereon, it fills his heart with
    delight.

Oh ! think of the danger of seafaring men
If any of these mighty mountains were falling on them;
Alas ! they would be killed ere the hand of man could them
    save
And, poor creatures, very likely find a watery grave !

'Tis most beautiful to see and hear the whales whistling and
    blowing,
And the sailors in their small boats quickly after them
    rowing,
While the whales keep lashing the water all their might
With their mighty tails, left and right.

In winter there's no sunlight there night or day,
Which, no doubt, will cause the time to pass tediously
    away,
And cause the Esquimaux to long for the light of day,
So as they will get basking themselves in the sun's bright
    array.

In summer there is perpetual sunlight,
Which fill the Esquimaux' hearts with delight;
And is seen every day and night in the blue sky,
Which makes the scenery appear most beautiful to the eye.

During summer and winter there the land is covered with
snow,
Which sometimes must fill the Esquimaux' hearts with woe
As they traverse fields of ice, ten of fifteen feet thick,
And with cold, no doubt, their hearts will be touched to
the quick.

And let those that read or hear this feel thankful to God
That the icy fields of Greenland they have never trod;
Especially while seated around the fireside on a cold winter
night,
Let them think of the cold and hardships Greenland sailors
have to fight.

JOTTINGS OF NEW YORK

A DESCRIPTIVE POEM

OH mighty City of New York! you are wonderful to
behold,
Your buildings are magnificent, the truth be it told,
They were the only thing that seemed to arrest my eye,
Because many of them are thirteen stories high.

And as for Central Park, it is lovely to be seen,
Especially in the summer season when its shrubberies and
trees are green;
And the Burns' statue is there to be seen,
Surrounded by trees, on the beautiful sward so green;
Also, Shakespeare and Sir Walter Scott,
Which by Englishmen and Scotchmen will ne'er be forgot.

There the people on the Sabbath-day in thousands resort,
All loud in conversation and searching for sport,
Some of them viewing the menagerie of wild beasts there,
And also beautiful black swans, I do declare.

And there's beautiful boats to be seen there,
And the joyous shouts of children do rend the air,
While the boats sail along them o'er Lohengrin Lake,
And the fare is five cents for children and adults ten is all
    they take.

And there's also summer-house shades and merry-go-
    rounds,
And with the merry laughter of children the Park resounds
During the livelong Sabbath-day,
Enjoying the merry-go-round play.

Then there's the elevated railroads, above five storeys high,
Which the inhabitants can see and hear night and day
    passing by,
Oh ! such a mass of people daily do throng,
No less than five hundred thousand daily pass along,
And all along the City you can get for five cents,
And, believe me, among the passengers there are few
    discontent.

And the tops of the houses are all flat,
And in the warm weather the people gather to chat,
Besides on the house-tops they dry their clothes,
And also many people all night on the house-tops repose.

And numerous ships and steamboats are there to be seen,
Sailing along the East River Water so green;
'Tis certainly a most beautiful sight
To see them sailing o'er the smooth water day and night.

And Brooklyn Bridge is a very great height,
And fills the stranger's heart with wonder at first sight,
But with all its loftiness, I venture to say,
For beauty it cannot surpass the new Railway Bridge of the
    Silvery Tay.

And there's also ten thousand rumsellers there,
Oh! wonderful to think, I do declare!
To accommodate the people of that city therein,
And to encourage them to commit all sorts of sin.

And on the Sabbath-day, ye will see many a man
Going for beer with a tin can,
And seems proud to be seen carrying home the beer
To treat his neighbours and family dear.

Then at night numbers of the people dance and sing,
Making the walls of their houses to ring
With their songs and dancing on Sabbath night,
Which I witnessed with disgust, and fled from the sight.

And with regard to New York and the sights I did see,
One street in Dundee is more worth to me,
And, believe me, the morning I sailed from New York
For Bonnie Dundee, my heart it felt as light as a cork.

A TRIBUTE TO MR MURPHY

AND THE BLUE RIBBON ARMY

ALL hail to Mr Murphy, he is a hero brave,
That has crossed the mighty Atlantic wave,
For what purpose let me pause and think—
I answer, to warn the people not to taste strong drink.

And, I'm sure, if they take his advice, they will never rue
The day they joined the Blue Ribbon Army in the year
    1882;
And I hope to their colours they will always prove true,
And shout, Hurrah! for Mr Murphy and the Ribbon of
    Blue.

What is strong drink? Let me think—I answer 'tis a thing
From whence the majority of evils spring,
And causes many a fireside with boisterous talk to ring,
And leaves behind it a deadly sting.

Some people do say it is good when taken in moderation,
But, when taken to excess, it leads to tribulation,
Also to starvation and loss of reputation,
Likewise your eternal soul's damnation.

The drunkard, he says he can't give it up,
For I confess temptation's in the cup;
But he wishes to God it was banished from the land,
While he holds the cup in his trembling hand.

And he exclaims in the agony of his soul—
Oh, God, I cannot myself control
From this most accurs'd cup!
Oh, help me, God, to give it up!

Strong drink to the body can do no good;
It defiles the blood, likewise the food,
And causes the drunkard with pain to groan,
Because it extracts the marrow from the bone:

And hastens him on to a premature grave,
Because to the cup he is bound a slave;
For the temptation is hard to thole,
And by it he will lose his immortal soul.

The more's the pity, I must say,
That so many men and women are by it led astray,
And decoyed from the paths of virtue and led on to vice
By drinking too much alcohol and acting unwise.

Good people all, of every degree,
I pray, ye all be warned by me:
I advise ye all to pause and think,
And never more to taste strong drink.

Because the drunkard shall never inherit the kingdom of
    God
And whosoever God loves he chastens with his rod :
Therefore, be warned, and think in time,
And don't drink any more whisky, rum, or wine.

But go at once—make no delay,
And join the Blue Ribbon Army without dismay,
And rally round Mr Murphy and make a bold stand,
And help to drive the Bane of Society from our land.

I wish Mr Murphy every success,
Hoping he will make rapid progress;
And to the Blue Ribbon Army may he always prove true,
And adhere to his colours—the beautiful blue.

FORGET-ME-NOT

A GALLANT knight and his betroth'd bride,
Were walking one day by a river side,
They talk'd of love, and the talk'd of war,
And how very foolish lovers are.

At length the bride to the knight did say,
There have been many young ladies led astray
By believing in all their lovers said,
And you are false to me I am afraid.

No, Ellen, I was never false to thee,
I never gave thee cause to doubt me;
I have always lov'd thee and do still,
And no other woman your place shall fill.

Dear Edwin, it may be true, but I am in doubt,
But there's some beautiful flowers here about,
Growing on the other side of the river,
But how to get one, I cannot discover.

Dear Ellen, they seem beautiful indeed,
But of them, dear, take no heed;
Because they are on the other side,
Besides, the river is deep and wide.

Dear Edwin, as I doubt your love to be untrue,
I ask one favour now from you :
Go ! fetch me a flower from across the river,
Which will prove you love me more than ever.

Dear Ellen ! I will try and fetch you a flower
If it lies within my power   *   *   *
To prove that I am true to you,
And what more can your Edwin do?

So he leap'd into the river wide,
And swam across to the other side,
To fetch a flower for his young bride,
Who watched him eagerly on the other side.

So he pluck'd a flower right merrily,
Which seemed to fill his heart with glee,
That it would please his lovely bride;
But, alas ! he never got to the other side.

For when he tried to swim across,
All power of his body he did loss,
But before he sank in the river wide,
He flung the flowers to his lovely bride.

And he cried, Oh, Heaven ! hard is my lot,
My dearest Ellen ! Forget me not :
For I was ever true to you,
My dearest Ellen ! I bid thee adieu !

Then she wrung her hands in wild despair,
Until her cries did rend the air;
And she cried, Edwin, dear, hard is our lot,
But I'll name their flower Forget-me-not.

And I'll remember thee while I live,
And to no other man my hand I'll give,
And I will place my affection on this little flower,
And it will solace me in a lonely hour.

THE ROYAL REVIEW

AUGUST 25, 1881

ALL hail to the Empress of India, Great Britain's Queen—
Long may she live in health, happy and serene—
That came from London, far away,
To view the Scottish Volunteers in grand array:
Most magnificent to be seen,
Near by Salisbury Crags and its pastures green,
Which will long be remembered by our gracious Queen—

And by the Volunteers, that came from far away,
Because it rain'd most of the day.
And with the rain their clothes were wet all through,
On the 25th day of August, at the Royal Review.
And to the Volunteers it was no lark,
Because they were ankle deep in mud in the Queen's Park,
Which proved to the Queen they were loyal and true,
To endure such hardships at the Royal Review.

Oh! it was a most beautiful scene
To see the Forfarshire Artillery marching past the Queen;
Her Majesty with their steady marching felt content,
Especially when their arms to her they did present.

And the Inverness Highland Volunteers seemed very gran',
And marched by steady to a man
Amongst the mud without dismay,
And the rain pouring down on them all the way.

And the bands they did play, God Save the Queen,
Near by Holyrood Palace and the Queen's Park so green.
Success to our noble Scottish volunteers!
I hoped they will be spared for many long years,
And to Her Majesty always prove loyal and true,
As they have done for the second time at the Royal Review.

To take them in general, they behaved very well,
The more that the rain fell on them pell-mell.
They marched by Her Majesty in very grand array,
Which will be remembered for many a long day,
Bidding defiance to wind and rain,
Which adds the more fame to their name.

And I hope none of them will have cause to rue
The day that they went to the Royal Review.
And I'm sure Her Majesty ought to feel proud,
And in their praise she cannot speak too loud,
Because the more that it did rain they did not mourn,
Which caused Her Majesty's heart with joy to burn,
Because she knew they were loyal and true
For enduring such hardships at the Royal Review.

THE BATTLE OF SHERIFFMUIR

A HISTORICAL POEM

'Twas in the year 1715, and on the 10th of November,
Which the people of Scotland have cause to remember;
On that day the Earl of Mar left Perth bound for
    Sheriffmuir,
At the same time leaving behind a garrison under Colonel
    Balfour.

Besides leaving a force of about three thousand men
    quartered in different parts of Fife,
To protect the people's property, and quell party strife,
The army along with him amounted to three thousand foot
    and twelve hundred cavalry,
All in the best of order, a most pleasant sight to see.

The two armies bivouacked near Sheriffmuir during the
    night,
And around their camp-fires they talked concerning the
    coming fight.
The Duke of Argyle's English army numbered eight
    thousand strong,
Besides four hundred horse, posted in the rear all along.

And the centre of the first line was composed of ten
    battalions of foot,
Consisting of four thousand, under the command of Clan-
    ranald and Glengarry to boot;
And at the head of these battalions Sir John Maclean and
    Brigadier Ogilvie,
And the two brothers of Sir Donald Macdonald of Sleat,
    all in high glee.

The Marquis of Huntly's squadron of horse was also there;
Likewise the Stirling squadron, carrying the Chevalier's
    standard, I do declare;
And the Pershshire squadron formed the left wing,
And with their boisterous shouts they made the welkin ring.

The centre of the second line consisted of eight battalions
    of infantry,
And three of the Earl of Seaforth's foot, famous for their
    bravery;
There were also two battalions of the Marquis of Huntly,
Besides the Earl of Panmure's battalion, all men of high
    degree.

And those of the Marquis of Tullibardine, commanded by
    the Viscount of Strathallan,
And of Logie Almond, and likewise Robertson of Strowan;
Besides two squadrons of horse under the Earl Marischal,
And the Angus squadron was on the left : these include
    them all.

During this formation, the Duke of Argyle was watching
    all the time,
But owing to the ground occupied by them he couldn't see
    their line,
Which was unfortunately obstructed by the brow of a hill,
At the thought thereof the Duke's heart with fear did fill.

The hill was occupied by a party of Earl Mar's troops
    looking towards Dunblane,
Which the Earl of Mar no doubt resolved to maintain;
Then the Duke returned to the army, and ordered the
    drums to beat,
But an hour elapsed before his army were ready Mar's to
    meet.

As soon as the Earl of Mars perceived Argyle's line was
    partially formed,
He gave orders that Argyle's army should be instantly
    stormed.
Then Mars placed himself at the head of the clans, and
    led forward his men,
As a noble hero would do, which no one can condemn.

Then he pulled off his hat, which he waved in his right
    hand,
And when he arrived within pistol-shot the Highlanders
    made a bold stand,
And they poured in a volley upon the English infantry,
And to the dismay of the Highlanders the English returned
    fire instantly.

And to the horror of the Highlanders Alan Muidartach
    was wounded mortally,
Then he was carried off the field, a most pitiful sight to see;
And as his men clustered around him they stood aghast,
And before he died he told them to hold their posts fast.

While lamenting the death of the Captain of Clanranald
    most pitifully,
Glengarry at this juncture sprang forward right manfully,
And throwing his bonnet into the air, he cried, heroically,
Revenge! revenge, revenge to-day! and mourning to-
    morrow ye shall see!

No sooner had he pronounced these words than the High-
    landers rushed forward, sword in hand,
Upon the royal battalions with the utmost fury, which they
    could not withstand,
And with their broadswords among the enemy they spread
    death and dismay,
Until the three battalions on Argyle's left wing instantly
    gave way.

Then a complete rout ensued, and the Earl of Mar pursued
    them half-a-mile;
Then he ordered his men to halt and rest a while,
Until he should put them into order right speedily,
Then follow the enemy at the double-march and complete
    the victory.

Then the Highlanders chased them and poured in a volley,
Besides they hewed them down with their broadswords
    mercilessly;
But somehow both armies got mixed together, and a
    general rout ensued,
While the Highlanders eagerly the English army hotly
    pursued.

The success on either side is doubtful to this day,
And all that can be said is, both armies ran away;

74

And on whichever side success lay it was toward the
   Government,
And to allay all doubts about which party won, we must
   feel content.

THE EXECUTION OF JAMES GRAHAM,
MARQUIS OF MONTROSE

A HISTORICAL POEM

'TWAS in the year of 1650, and on the twenty-first of May,
The city of Edinburgh was put into a state of dismay
By the noise of drums and trumpets, which on the air arose,
That the great sound attracted the notice of Montrose.

Who enquired at the Captain of the guard the cause of it,
Then the officer told him, as he thought most fit,
That the Parliament dreading an attempt might be made
   to rescue him,
The soldiers were called out to arms, and that had made
   the din.

Do I, said Montrose, continue such a terror still?
Now when these good men are about my blood to spill,
But let them look to themselves, for after I am dead,
Their wicked consciences will be in continual dread.

After partaking of a hearty breakfast, he commenced his
   toilet,
Which, in his greatest trouble, he seldom did forget.
And while in the act of combing his hair,
He was visited by the Clerk Register, who made him stare,

When he told him he shouldn't be so particular with his
   head,
For in a few hours he would be dead;

But Montrose replied, While my head is my own I'll dress
    it at my ease,
And to-morrow, when it becomes yours, treat it as you
    please.

He was waited upon by the Magistrates of the city,
But, alas! for him they had no pity.
He was habited in a superb cloak, ornamented with gold
    and silver lace;
And before the hour of execution an immense assemblage
    of people were round the place.

From the prison, bareheaded, in a cart, they conveyed him
    along the Watergate
To the place of execution on the High Street, where about
    thirty thousand people did wait,
Some crying and sighing, a most pitiful sight to see,
All waiting patiently to see the executioner hang Montrose,
    a man of high degree.

Around the place of execution, all of them were deeply
    affected,
But Montrose, the noble hero, seemed not the least
    dejected;
And when on the scaffold he had, says his biographer
    Wishart,
Such a grand air and majesty, which made the people start.

As the fatal hour was approaching when he had to bid the
    world adieu,
He told the executioner to make haste and get quickly
    through,
But the executioner smiled grimly, but spoke not a word,
Then he tied the Book of Montrose's Wars round his neck
    with a cord.

Then he told the executioner his foes would remember him
    hereafter,

And he was as well pleased as if his Majesty had made him
    Knight of the Garter;
Then he asked to be allowed to cover his head,
But he was denied permission, yet he felt no dread.

Then he asked leave to keep on his cloak,
But was also denied, which was a most grievous stroke;
Then he told the Magistrates, if they could invent any more
    tortures for him,
He would endure them all for the cause he had suffered,
    and think it no sin.

On arriving at the top of the ladder with great firmness,
His heroic appearance greatly did the bystanders impress,
Then Montrose asked the executioner how long his body
    would be suspended,
Three hours was the answer, but Montrose was not the
    least offended.

Then he presented the executioner with three or four pieces
    of gold,
Whom he freely forgave, to his honour be it told,
And told him to throw him off as soon as he uplifted his
    hands,
While the executioner watched the fatal signal, and in
    amazement stands.

And on the noble patriot raising his hands, the executioner
    began to cry,
Then quickly he pulled the rope down from the gibbet on
    high,
And around Montrose's neck he fixed the rope very gently,
And in an instant the great Montrose was launched into
    eternity.

Then the spectators expressed their disapprobation by a
    general groan,
And they all dispersed quietly, and wended their way home,
And his bitterest enemies that saw his death that day,

Their hearts were filled with sorrow and dismay.

Thus died, at the age of thirty-eight, James Graham,
    Marquis of Montrose,
Who was brought to a premature grave by his bitter foes;
A commander who had acquired great military glory
In a short space of time, which cannot be equalled in story.

ROBERT BURNS

Immortal Robert Burns of Ayr,
There's but few poets can with you compare;
Some of your poems and songs are very fine :
To "Mary in Heaven" is most sublime;
And then again in your "Cottar's Saturday Night,"
Your genius there does shine most bright,
As pure as the dewdrops of night.

Your "Tam o' Shanter is very fine,
Both funny, racy, and divine,
From John o' Groats to Dumfries
All critics consider it to be a masterpiece,
And also, you have said the same,
Therefore they are not to blame.

And in my own opinion both you and they are right,
For your genius there does sparkle bright,
Which I most solemnly declare
To thee, Immortal Bard of Ayr!

Your "Banks and Braes of Bonnie Doon"
Is sweet and melodious in its tune,
And the poetry is moral and sublime,
And in my opinion nothing can be more fine.

Your "Scots wha hae wi' Wallace bled"
Is most beautiful to hear sung or read;

For your genius there does shine as bright,
Like unto the stars of night . . . . .

Immortal Bard of Ayr! I must conclude, my muse
To speak in praise of thee does not refuse,
For you were a mighty poet, few could with you compare,
And also an honour to Scotland, for your genius it is rare.

A TALE OF THE SEA

A PATHETIC tale of the sea I will unfold,
Enough to make one's blood run cold;
Concerning four fishermen cast adrift in a dory.
As I've been told, I'll relate the story.

'Twas on the 8th April, on the afternoon of that day,
That the little village of Louisburg was thrown into a wild
    state of dismay,
And the villagers flew to the beach in a state of wild uproar
And in a dory they found four men were cast ashore.

Then the villagers, in surprise, assembled about the dory,
And they found that the bottom of the boat was gory;
Then their hearts were seized with sudden dread,
When they discovered that two of the men were dead.

And the two survivors were exhausted from exposure,
    hunger, and cold,
Which caused the spectators to shudder when them they
    did behold;
And with hunger the poor men couldn't stand on their feet,
They felt so weakly on their legs for want of meat.

They were carried to a boarding-house without delay,
But those that were looking on were stricken with dismay,
When the remains of James and Angus M'Donald were
    found in the boat,

Likewise three pieces of flesh in a pool of blood afloat.

Angus M'Donald's right arm was missing from the elbow,
And the throat was cut in a sickening manner, which filled
    the villagers hearts with woe,
Especially when they saw two pieces of flesh had been cut
    from each thigh,
'Twas then the kind-hearted villagers did murmur and sigh.

Angus M'Donald must have felt the pangs of hunger
    before he did try
To cut two pieces from James M'Donald's thigh;
But, Oh, heaven! the pangs of hunger are very hard to
    thole,
And anything that's eatable is precious unto a hungry soul.

Alas! it is most pitiful and horrible to think,
That with hunger Christians will each other's blood drink,
And each each other's flesh to save themselves from
    starvation;
But the pangs of hunger makes them mad, and drives them
    to desperation.

An old American soldier, that had passed through the
    Civil War,
Declared the scene surpassed anything he's seen by far,
And at the sight, the crowd in horror turned away,
Which no doubt they will remember for many a day.

Colin Chisholm, one of the survivors, was looking very
    pale,
Stretched on a sofa, at the boarding-house, making his
    wail;
Poor fellow! his feet were greatly swollen, and with a
    melancholy air,
He gave the following account of the distressing affair:

We belonged to the American fishing schooner, named
    "Cicely,"

And our captain was a brave man, called M'Kenzie;
And the vessel had fourteen hands altogether,
And during the passage we had favourable weather.

'Twas on March the 17th we sailed from Gloucester, on the
      Wednesday,
And all our hearts felt buoyant and gay;
And we arrived on the Western banks on the succeeding
      Tuesday,
While the time unto us seemed to pass merrily away.

About eight o'clock in the morning, we left the vessel in a
      dory,
And I hope all kind Christians will take heed to my story:
Well, while we were at work, the sky began to frown,
And with a dense fog we were suddenly shut down.

Then we hunted and shouted, and every nerve did strain,
Thinking to find our schooner, but, alas! it was all in vain:
Because the thick fog hid the vessel from our view,
And to keep ourselves warm we closely to each other drew.

We had not one drop of water, nor provisions of any kind,
Which, alas! soon began to tell on our mind;
Especially upon James M'Donald, who was very thinly
      clad,
And with the cold and hunger he felt almost mad.

And looking from the stern where he was lying,
He said, Good-bye, mates, Oh! I am dying!
Poor fellow, we kept his body, thinking the rest of us
      would be saved,
Then, with hunger, Angus M'Donald began to cry and
      madly raved.

And he cried, Oh, God! send us some kind of meat,
Because I'm resolved to have something to eat;
Oh! do not let us starve on the briny flood,
Or else I will drink of poor Jim's blood.

Then he suddenly seized his knife and cut off poor Jim's
  arm,
Not thinking in his madness he'd done any harm;
Then poor Jim's blood he did drink, and his flesh did eat,
Declaring that the blood tasted like cream, and was a treat.

Then he asked me to taste it, saying, It was good without
  doubt,
Then I tasted it, but in disgust I instantly spat it out;
Saying, If I was to die within an hour on the briny flood,
I would neither eat the flesh nor drink the blood.

Then in the afternoon again he turned to me,
Saying, I'm going to cut Jim's throat for more blood d'ye
  see;
Then I begged of him, for God's sake, not to cut the
  throat of poor Jim,
But he cried, Ha! ha! to save my own life I consider it no
  sin.
I tried to prevent him, but he struck me without dismay,
And cut poor Jim's throat in defiance of me, or all I could
  say,
Also a piece of flesh from each thigh, and began to eat
  away,
But poor fellow he sickened about noon, and died on the
  Sunday.

Now it is all over, and I will thank God all my life,
Who has preserved me and my mate, M'Eachern, in the
  midst of danger and strife;
And I hope that all landsmen of low and high degree,
Will think of the hardships of poor mariners while at sea.

DESCRIPTIVE JOTTINGS OF LONDON

As I stood upon London Bridge and viewed the mighty
  throng

Of thousands of people in cabs and 'busses rapidly
    whirling along,
All furiously driving to and fro,
Up one street and down another as quick as they could go:

Then I was struck with the discordant sounds of human
    voices there,
Which seemed to me like wild geese cackling in the air:
And the river Thames is a most beautiful sight,
To see the steamers sailing upon it by day and by night.

And the Tower of London is most gloomy to behold,
And the crown of England lies there, begemmed with
    precious stones and gold;
King Henry the Sixth was murdered there by the Duke of
    Glo'ster,
And when he killed him with his sword he called him an
    imposter.
St. Paul's Cathedral is the finest building that ever I did
    see,
There's no building can surpass it in the city of Dundee,
Because it's magnificent to behold,
With its beautiful dome and spire glittering like gold.

And as for Nelson's monument that stands in Trafalgar
    Square,
It is a most stately monument I most solemnly declare,
And towering defiantly very high,
Which arrests strangers' attention while passing by.

Then there's two beautiful water-fountains spouting up
    very high,
Where the weary traveller can drink when he feels dry;
And at the foot of the monument there's three bronze
    lions in grand array,
Enough to make the stranger's heart throb with dismay.

Then there's Mr Spurgeon, a great preacher, which no one
    dare gainsay,

I went to hear him preach on the Sabbath-day,
And he made my heart feel light and gay,
When I heard him preach and pray.

And the Tabernacle was crowded from ceiling to floor,
And many were standing outside the door;
He is an eloquent preacher I honestly declare,
And I was struck with admiration as on him I did stare.

Then there's Petticoat Lane I venture to say,
It's a wonderful place on the Sabbath-day;
There wearing-apparel can be bought to suit the young
or old,
For the ready cash, silver, coppers, or gold.

Oh! mighty city of London, you are wonderful to see,
And thy beauties no doubt fill the tourist's heart with glee;
But during my short stay, and while wandering there,
Mr Spurgeon was the only man I heard speaking proper
English I do declare.

BURNING OF THE EXETER THEATRE

'Twas in the year of 1887, which many people will long
remember,
The burning of the Theatre at Exeter on the 5th of
September,
Alas! that ever-to-be-remembered and unlucky night,
When one hundred and fifty lost their lives, a most
agonising sight.

The play on this night was called "Romany Rye,"
And at act four, scene third, Fire! Fire! was the cry;
And all in a moment flames were seen issuing from the
stage,
Then the women screamed frantically, like wild beasts in
a cage.

84

Then a panic ensued, and each one felt dismayed,
And from the burning building a rush was made;
And soon the theatre was filled with a blinding smoke,
So that the people their way out had to grope.

The shrieks of those trying to escape were fearful to hear,
Especially the cries of those who had lost their friends most
    dear;
Oh, the scene was most painful in the London Inn Square,
To see them ringing their hands and tearing their hair!

And as the flames spread, great havoc they did make,
And the poor souls fought heroically in trying to make
    their escape;
Oh, it was horrible to see men and women trying to reach
    the door!
But in many cases death claimed the victory, and their
    struggles were o'er.

Alas! 'twas pitiful the shrieks of the audience to hear,
Especially as the flames to them drew near;
Because on every face were depicted despair and woe,
And many of them jumped from their windows into the
    street below.

The crushed and charred bodies were carried into London
    Hotel yard,
And to alleviate their sufferings the doctors tried hard;
But, alas! their attendance on many was thrown away,
But those that survived were conveyed to Exeter Hospital
    without delay.

And all those that had their wounds dressed proceeded
    home,
Accompanied by their friends, and making a loud moan;
While the faces and necks of others were sickening to
    behold,
Enough to chill one's blood, and make the heart turn cold.

Alas! words fail to describe the desolation,
And in many homes it will cause great lamentation;
Because human remains are beyond all identification,
Which will cause the relatives of the sufferers to be in great
  tribulation.

Oh, Heaven! it must have been an awful sight,
To see the poor souls struggling hard with all their might,
Fighting hard their lives to save,
While many in the smoke and burning flame did madly
  rave!

It was the most sickening sight that ever anybody saw,
Human remains, beyond recognition, covered with a heap
  of straw;
And here and there a body might be seen, and a maimed
  hand,
Oh, such a sight, that the most hard-hearted person could
  hardly withstand!

The number of people in the theatre was between seven
  and eight thousand,
But, alas! one hundred and fifty by the fire have been
  found dead;
And the most lives were lost on the stairs leading from the
  gallery,
And these were roasted to death, which was sickening to
  see.

The funerals were conducted at the expense of the local
  authority,
And two hours and more elapsed at the mournful cere-
  mony;
And at one grave there were two thousand people, a very
  great crowd,
And most of the men were bareheaded and weeping aloud.

Alas! many poor children have been bereft of their fathers
  and mothers,

86

Who will be sorely missed by little sisters and brothers;
But, alas! unto them they can ne'er return again,
Therefore the poor little innocents must weep for them in
vain.

I hope all kind Christian souls will help the friends of the
dead,
Especially those that have lost the winners of their bread;
And if they do, God surely will them bless,
Because pure Christianity is to help the widows and
orphans in distress.

I am very glad to see Henry Irving had sent a hundred
pound,
And I hope his brother actors will subscribe their mite all
round;
And if they do it will add honour to their name,
Because whatever is given towards a good cause they will
it regain.

GENERAL GORDON,
THE HERO OF KHARTOUM

ALAS! now o'er the civilised world there hangs a gloom
For brave General Gordon, that was killed in Khartoum;
He was a Christian hero, and a soldier of the Cross,
And to England his death will be a very great loss.

He was very cool in temper, generous and brave,
The friend of the poor, the sick, and the slave;
And many a poor boy he did educate,
And laboured hard to do so both early and late.

He was a man that did not care for worldly gear,
Because the living and true God he did fear;
And the hearts of the poor he liked to cheer,
And by his companions in arms he was loved most dear.

He always took the Bible for his guide,
And he liked little boys to walk by his side;
He preferred their company more so than men,
Because he knew there was less guile in them.

And in his conversation he was modest and plain,
Denouncing all pleasures he considered sinful and vain,
And in battle he carried no weapon but a small cane,
Whilst the bullets fell around him like a shower of rain.

He burned the debtors' books that were imprisoned in
    Khartoum,
And freed them from a dismal prison gloom,
Those that were imprisoned for debt they couldn't pay,
And sent them rejoicing on their way.

While engaged in the Russian war, in the midst of the fight,
He stood upon a rising ground and viewed them left and
    right,
But for their shot and shell he didn't care a jot,
While the officers cried, Gordon, come down, or else you'll
    be shot.

His cane was christened by the soldiers Gordon's wand of
    victory,
And when he waved it the soldiers' hearts were filled with
    glee,
While with voice and gesture he encouraged them in the
    strife,
And he himself appeared to possess a charmed life.
Once when leading a storming party the soldiers drew
    back,
But he quickly observed that courage they did lack,
Then he calmly lighted a cigar, and turned cheerfully
    round,
And the soldiers rushed boldly on with a bound.

And they carried the position without delay,
And the Chinese rebels soon gave way,

Because God was with him during the day,
And with those that trust Him for ever and aye.

He was always willing to conduct meetings for the poor,
And meat and clothing for them he tried to procure,
And he always had little humourous speeches at command,
And to hear him deliver them it must have been grand.

In military life his equal could not be found,
No! if you were to search the wide world around,
And 'tis pitiful to think he has met with such a doom
By a base *traitor knave* while in Khartoum.

Yes, the black-hearted traitor opened the gates of Khar-
    toum,
And through that the Christian hero has met his doom,
For when the gates were opened the Arabs rushed madly in,
And foully murdered him while they laughingly did grin.

But he defended himself nobly with axe and sword in hand,
But, alas! he was soon overpowered by that savage band,
And his body received a hundred spear wounds and more,
While his murderers exultingly did loudly shriek and roar.

But heaven's will, 'tis said, must be done,
And according to his own opinion his time was come;
But I hope he is now in heaven reaping his reward.
Although his fate on earth was really very hard.

I hope the people will his memory revere,
And take an example from him, and worship God in fear,
And never be too fond of worldly gear,
And walk in General Gordon's footsteps while they are
    here.

THE TRAGIC DEATH OF
THE REV. A. H. MACKONOCHIE

Friends of humanity, of high and low degree,
I pray ye all come listen to me;
And truly I will relate to ye,
The tragic fate of the Rev. Alexander Heriot Mackonochie.

Who was on a visit to the Bishop of Argyle
For the good of his health, for a short while;
Because for the last three years his memory had been
    affected
Which prevented him from getting his thoughts collected.

'Twas on Thursday, the 15th of December, in the year of
    1887,
He left the Bishop's house to go and see Loch Leven;
And he was accompanied by a little skye terrier and a
    deerhound,
Besides the Bishop's two dogs, that knew well the ground.

And as he had taken the same walk the day before,
The Bishop's mind was undisturbed and easy on that score;
Besides the Bishop had been told by some men
That they saw him making his way up a glen.

From which a great river flows down with a mighty roar,
From the great mountains of the Mamore;
And this route led him towards trackless wastes eastward,
And no doubt to save his life he had struggled very hard.

And as Mr Mackonochie had not returned at dinner time,
The Bishop ordered two men to search for him, which they
    didn't decline;
Then they searched for him along the road he should have
    returned,
But when they found him not, they sadly mourned.

And when the Bishop heard it, he procured a carriage and
    pair,
While his heart was full of woe, and in a state of despair;
He organised three search parties without delay,
And headed one of the parties in person without dismay.

And each party searched in a different way,
But to their regret at the end of the day;
Most unfortunately no discovery had been made,
Then they lost hope of finding him, and began to be
    afraid.

And as a last hope, two night searches were planned,
And each party with well lighted lamps in hand
Started on their perilous mission, Mr Mackonochie to try
    and find,
In the midst of the driving hail, and the howling wind.

One party searched a distant sporting lodge with right good
    will,
Besides through brier, and bush, and snow, on the hill;
And the Bishop's party explored the Devil's Staircase with
    hearts full of woe,
A steep pass between the Kinloch hills, and the hills of
    Glencoe.

Oh ! it was a pitch dark and tempestuous night,
And the searchers would have lost their way without lamp
    light;
But the brave searchers stumbled along for hours, but slow,
Over rocks, and ice, and sometimes through deep snow.

And as the Bishop's party were searching they met a third
    party from Glencoe side,
Who had searched bracken and burn, and the country
    wide;
And sorrow was depicted in each one's face,
Because of the Rev. Mr Mackonochie they could get no
trace.

But on Saturday morning the Bishop set off again
Hoping that the last search wouldn't prove in vain;
Accompanied by a crowd of men and dogs,
All resolved to search the forest and the bogs.

And the party searched with might and main,
Until they began to think their search would prove in vain;
When the Bishop's faithful dogs raised a pitiful cry,
Which was heard by the searchers near by.

Then the party pressed on right manfully,
And sure enough there were the dogs guarding the body
   of Mackonochie;
And the corpse was cold and stiff, having been long dead,
Alas! almost frozen, and a wreath of snow around the head.

And as the searchers gathered round the body in pity they
   did stare,
Because his right foot was stained with blood, and bare;
But when the Bishop o'er the corpse had offered up a
   prayer,
He ordered his party to carry the corpse to his house on a
   bier.

So a bier of sticks was most willingly and quickly made,
Then the body was most tenderly upon it laid;
And they bore the corpse and laid inside the Bishop's
   private chapel,
Then the party took one sorrowful look and bade the
   corpse, farewell.

THE WRECK OF THE WHALER "OSCAR"

'Twas on the 1st of April, and in the year of Eighteen
   thirteen,
That the whaler "Ocar" was wrecked not far from Aber-
   deen;

92

'Twas all of a sudden the wind arose, and a terrific blast
it blew,
And the "Oscar" was lost, and forty-two of a gallant crew.

The storm burst forth with great violence, but of short
duration,
And spread o'er a wide district, and filled the people's
hearts with consternation,
And its effects were such that the people will long mind,
Because at Peterhead the roof was torn off a church by the
heavy wind.

The "Oscar" joined other four ships that were lying in
Aberdeen Bay,
All ready to start for Greenland without delay,
While the hearts of each ship's crew felt light and gay,
But, when the storm burst upon them, it filled their hearts
with dismay.

The wind had been blowing westerly during the night,
But suddenly it shifted to the North-east, and blew with all
its might,
And thick and fast fell the blinding snow,
Which filled the poor sailors' hearts with woe.

And the "Oscar" was exposed to the full force of the gale,
But the crew resolved to do their best, allowing they should
fail,
So they weighed anchor, and stood boldly out for sea,
While the great crowds that had gathered cheered them
encouragingly.

The ill-fated "Oscar," however, sent a boat ashore
For some of her crew that were absent, while the angry
sea did roar,
And 'twas with difficulty the men got aboard,
And to make the ship alright they wrought with one
accord.

Then suddenly the wind shifted, and a treacherous calm
    ensued,
And the vessel's deck with snow was thickly strewed;
And a heavy sea was running with a strong flood tide,
And it soon became apparent the men wouldn't be able
    the ship to guide.

And as the "Oscar" drifted further and further to leeward,
The brave crew tried hard her backward drifting to retard,
But all their efforts proved in vain, for the storm broke out
    anew,
While the drifting snow hid her from the spectators' view.

And the position of the "Oscar" was critical in the
    extreme,
And as the spray washed o'er the vessel, O what a soul-
    harrowing scene!
And notwithstanding the fury of the gale and the blinding
    snow,
Great crowds watched the "Oscar" as she was tossed to and
    fro.

O heaven! it was a most heart-rending sight
To see the crew struggling against wind and blinding snow
    with all their might,
While the mighty waves lashed her sides and angry did
    roar,
Which to their relatives were painful to see that were
    standing on shore,

All eagerly watching her attempt to ride out the storm,
Especially their friends and relatives, who seemed very
    forlorn,
Because the scene was awe-inspiring and made them stand
    aghast,
For every moment seemed to be the "Oscar's" last.

Oh! it was horrible to see the good ship in distress,
Battling hard against wind and tide to clear the Girdleness,

A conspicuous promontory on the south side of Aberdeen
    Bay,
Where many a stout ship and crew have gone down
    passing that way.

At last the vessel was driven ashore in the bay of Greyhope,
And the "Oscar" with the elements no longer could cope.
While the big waves lashed her furiously, and she received
    fearful shocks,
Until a mighty wave hurled her among large boulders of
    rocks.

And when the vessel struck, the crew stood aghast,
But they resolved to hew down the mainmast,
Which the spectators watched with eager interest,
And to make it fall on the rocks the brave sailors tried their
    best.

But, instead of falling on the rocks, it dropped into the
    angry tide,
Then a groan arose from those that were standing on the
    shore side;
And the mainmast in its fall brought down the foremast,
Then all hope of saving the crew seemed gone at last.

And a number of the crew were thrown into the boiling
    surge below,
While loud and angry the stormy wind did blow,
And the good ship was dashed to pieces from stern to stem,
Within a yard or two of their friends, who were powerless
    to save them.

Oh! it was an appalling sight to see the "Oscar" in
    distress,
While to the forecastle was seen clinging brave Captain
    Innes
And five of a crew, crying for help, which none could
    afford,

Alas! poor fellows, crying aloud to God with one accord!
But their cry to God for help proved all in vain,
For the ship and men sank beneath the briny main,
And out of a crew of forty-four men, only two were saved,
But, landsmen, think how manfully that unfortunate crew
   behaved.

And also think of the mariners while you lie down to sleep,
And pray to God to protect them while on the briny deep,
For their hardships are many, and hard to endure,
There's only a plank between them and a watery grave,
   which makes their lives unsure.

THE HORRORS OF MAJUBA

'Twas after the great Majuba fight:
And the next morning, at daylight,
Captain Macbean's men were ordered to headquarters
   camp,
So immediately Captain Macbean and his men set out on
   tramp.

And they were joined by the Blue Jackets and 58th men,
Who, for unflinching courage, no man can them condemn;
And that brave little band was commissioned to bury their
   dead,
And the little band numbered in all about one hundred.

And they were supplied with a white flag, fit emblem of
   death,
Then they started off to O'Neill's farm, with bated breath,
Where their comrades had been left the previous night,
And were lying weltering in their gore, oh! what a horrible
   sight.

And when they arrived at the foot of Majuba Hill,

They were stopped by a Boer party, but they meant no ill,
Who asked them what they wanted without dismay,
And when they said, their dead, there was no further delay.

Then the brave heroes marched on, without any dread,
To the Hill of Majuba to collect and bury their dead;
And to see them climbing Majuba it was a fearful sight,
And much more so on a dark pitch night.

And on Majuba there was a row of dead men,
Numbering about forty or fifty of them;
There were also numbers of wounded men lying on the
    ground,
And when Captain Macbean's party gazed on them their
    sorrow was profound.

Oh, heaven! what a sight of blood and brains!
While the grass was red all o'er with blood-stains;
Especially at the edge of the Hill, where the 92nd men
    were killed,
'Twas there that the eyes of Macbean's party with tears
    filled,

When they saw their dead and dying comrades in arms,
Who were always foremost in the fight during war's alarms;
But who were now lying on Majuba Hill,
And, alas! beyond the aid of all human skill.

Then they went about two hundred yards down the Hill,
And collected fourteen more bodies, which made their
    blood run chill;
And, into one grave, seventy-five bodies they buried there,
All mostly 92nd men, who, I hope, are free from all care.

Oh! think of that little gallant British band,
Who, at Majuba, made such a heroic stand,
And, take them altogether, they behaved like brave men,
But, alas! they were slaughtered like sheep in a pen.

Poor fellows ! there were few of them left to retire,
Because undauntedly they faced that murderous fire,
That the mighty host poured in upon them, left and right,
From their numerous rifles, day and night.

The conduct of the 92nd was most brave throughout,
Which has always been the case, without any doubt;
At least, it has been the case in general with the Highland
    Brigade,
Because in the field they are the foremost, and seldom
    afraid.

And to do the British justice at Majuba they behaved right
    well,
But by overwhelming numbers the most of them fell,
Which I'm very sorry to relate,
That such a brave little band met with such a fate.

The commanders and officers deserve great praise,
Because they told their men to hold Majuba for three
    days;
And so they did, until the most of them fell,
Fighting nobly for their Queen and country they loved
    right well.

But who's to blame for their fate I'm at a loss to know,
But I think 'twas by fighting too numerous a foe;
But there's one thing I know, and, in conclusion, will say,
That their fame will be handed down to posterity for many
    a day !

THE DESTROYING ANGEL

OR THE POET'S DREAM

I DREAMT a dream the other night
That an Angel appeared to me, clothed in white.

Oh! it was a beautiful sight,
Such as filled my heart with delight.

And in her hand she held a flaming branu,
Which she waved above her head most grand;
And on me she glared with love-beaming eyes,
Then she commanded me from my bed to arise.

And in a sweet voice she said, "You must follow me,
And in a short time you shall see
The destruction of all the public-houses in the city,
Which is, my friend, the God of Heaven's decree."

Then from my bed in fear I arose,
And quickly donned on my clothes;
And when that was done she said, "Follow me
Direct to the High Street, fearlessly."

So with the beautiful Angel away I did go,
And when we arrived at the High Street, Oh! what a show;
I suppose there were about five thousand men there,
All vowing vengeance against the publicans, I do declare.

Then the Angel cried with a solemn voice aloud
To that vast and Godly assembled crowd,
"Gentlemen belonging to the fair City of Dundee,
Remember I have been sent here by God to warn ye

"That by God's decree ye must take up arms and follow me
And wreck all the public-houses in this fair City,
Because God cannot countenance such dens of iniquity.
Therefore, friends of God, come, follow me.

"Because God had said there's no use preaching against
    strong drink,
Therefore, by taking up arms against it, God does think,
That is the only and the effectual cure
To banish it from the land, He is quite sure.

"Besides, it has been denounced in Dundee for fifty years
By the friends of Temperance, while oft they have shed
tears.
Therefore, God thinks there's no use denouncing it any
longer,
Because the more that's said against it seemingly it grows
stronger."

And while the Angel was thus addressing the people,
The Devil seemed to be standing on the Townhouse Steeple,
Foaming at the mouth with rage, and seemingly much
annoyed,
And kicking the Steeple because the public-houses were
going to be destroyed.

Then the Angel cried, "Satan, avaunt! begone!"
Then he vanished in the flame, to the amazement of
everyone,
And waving aloft the flaming brand
That she carried in her right hand

She cried, "Now, friends of the Temperance cause, follow
me :
For remember it's God's high decree
To destroy all the public-houses in this fair City;
Therefore, friends of God, let's commence this war immedi-
ately."

Then from the High Street we all did retire,
As the Angel, sent by God, did desire;
And along the Perth Road we all did go,
While the Angel set fire to the public-houses along that row.

And when the Perth Road public-houses were fired, she
cried, "Follow me,
And next I'll fire the Hawkhill public-houses instantly."
Then away we went with the Angel, without dread or woe,
And she fired the Hawkhill public houses as onward we
did go.

Then she cried, "Let's on to the Scouringburn, in God's
  name."
And away to the Scouringburn we went, with our hearts
  aflame,
As the destroying Angel did command.
And when there she fired the public- houses, which looked
  very grand.

And when the public-houses they were blazing like a kiln,
She cried, "Now, my friends, we'll march to the Bonnet
  Hill,
And we'll fire the dens of iniquity without dismay,
Therefore let's march on, my friends, without delay."

And when we arrived at the Bonnet Hill,
The Angel fired the public-houses, as she did well.
Then she cried, "We'll leave them now to their fate,
And march on to the Murraygate."

Then we marched on to the Murraygate,
And the Angel fired the public-houses there, a most
  deserving fate.
Then to the High Street we marched and fired them there,
Which was a most beautiful blaze, I do declare.

And on the High Street, old men and women were gathered
  there,
And as the flames ascended upwards, in amazement they
  did stare
When they saw the public-houses in a blaze,
But they clapped their hands with joy and to God gave
  praise.

Then the Angel cried, "Thank God, Christ's Kingdom's
  near at hand,
And there will soon be peace and plenty throughout the
  land,
And the ravages of demon Drink no more will be seen."
But, alas, I started up in bed, and behold it was a dream!

LINES IN DEFENCE OF THE STAGE

Good people of high and low degree,
I pray ye all be advised by me,
And don't believe what the clergy doth say,
That by going to the theatre you will be led astray.

No, in the theatre we see vice punished and virtue
   rewarded,
The villain either hanged or shot, and his career retarded;
Therefore the theatre is useful in every way,
And has no inducement to lead the people astray.

Because therein we see the end of the bad man,
Which must appal the audience—deny it who can—
Which will help to retard them from going astray,
While witnessing in a theatre a moral play.

The theatre ought to be encouraged in every respect,
Because example is better than precept,
And is bound to have a greater effect
On the minds of theatre-goers in every respect.

Sometimes in theatres, guilty creatures there have been
Struck to the soul by the cunning of the scene;
By witnessing a play wherein murder is enacted,
They were proven to be murderers, they felt so distracted.

And left the theatre, they felt so much fear,
Such has been the case, so says Shakespeare.
And such is my opinion, I will venture to say,
That murderers will quake with fear on seeing murder in a
   play.

Hamlet discovered his father's murderer by a play
That he composed for the purpose, without dismay,
And the king, his uncle, couldn't endure to see that play,
And he withdrew from the scene without delay.

And by that play the murder was found out,
And clearly proven, without any doubt;
Therefore, stage representation has a greater effect
On the minds of the people than religious precept.

We see in Shakespeare's tragedy of Othello, which is
    sublime,
Cassio losing his lieutenancy through drinking wine;
And, in delirium and grief, he exclaims—
"Oh, that men should put an enemy in their mouths to
    steal away their brains!"

A young man in London went to the theatre one night
To see the play of George Barnwell, and he got a great
    fright;
He saw George Barnwell murder his uncle in the play,
And he had resolved to murder his uncle, but was stricken
    with dismay.

But when he saw George Barnwell was to be hung
The dread of murdering his uncle tenaciously to him clung,
That he couldn't murder and rob his uncle dear,
Because the play he saw enacted filled his heart with fear.

And, in conclusion, I will say without dismay,
Visit the theatre without delay,
Because the theatre is a school of morality,
And hasn't the least tendency to lead to prodigality.

THE BLACK WATCH MEMORIAL

YE Sons of Mars, it gives me great content
To think there has been erected a handsome monument
In memory of the Black Watch, which is magnificent to
    see,
Where they first were embodied at Aberfeldy.

And as a Highland regiment they are worthy of what has
    been done for them,
Because a more courageous regiment we cannot find of men
Who have bravely fought and bled in defence of their
    country,
Especially in the Russian War and Soudan War they made
    their enemies flee.

The monument I hope will stand secure for many a long
    day,
And may the people of Aberfeldy always feel gay;
As they gaze upon the beautiful Black Watch monument,
I hope they will think of the brave soldiers and feel content.

'Twas in the year of 1887, and on Saturday the 12th of
    November,
Which the people of Aberfeldy and elsewhere will
    remember,
Who came all the way from Edinburgh, Glasgow, Perth
    and Dundee,
Besides the Pitlochry Volunteers headed the procession right
    manfully.

And the Perthshire Rifles joined the procession with their
    pipe band.
Then followed a detachment of the 42nd Highlanders so
    grand,
Under the command of Lieutenant McLeod,
Whose duty it was to represent the regiment of which he
    felt proud.

The pipe band of the Glasgow Highlanders also were there,
And Taymouth Brass Band, which discoursed sweet music
    I do declare;
Also military officers and the magistrates of Aberfeldy,
While in the rear came the members of Committee.

There were also Freemasons, Foresters, all in a row,

And wearing their distinctive regalias, which made a great
show;
And the processionists were formed into three sides of a
square
Around the monument, while the music of the bands did
rend the air.

The noble Marquis of Breadalbane arrived on the ground
at 1.30,
Escorted by a guard of honour and his pipe band;
Then the bands struck up, and the pipes were set a
bumming,
And all with one accord played up the "Campbell's are
Coming."

Then his Lordship ascended a platform on the north side
of the monument,
And the bands played cheerfully till their breath was almost
spent;
Then his Lordship received three ringing cheers from the
people there,
Then he requested the Rev. John M'Lean to open the
proceedings with prayer.

And after the prayer, Major Menzies stepped forward
And said, "Ladies and gentlemen, for the Black Watch I
have great regard;
And the duty I have to perform gives me great content,
And that is to ask the noble Marquis to unveil this
monument."

Then he handed the noble Marquis a Lochaber axe to
unveil the Monument,
And the Marquis said, "Sir, to your request I most willingly
consent."
Then he unveiled the monument in memory of the gallant
Forty-twa,
While the bands played up the "Highland Laddie" as loud
as they could blaw.

And when the bands ceased playing the noble Marquis said,
"This monument I declare is very elegantly made,
And its bold style is quite in keeping with the country I
find,
And the Committee were fortunate in obtaining so able a
designer as Mr Rhind."

Then, turning to the Chief Magistrate of Aberfeldy,
He said, "Sir, I have been requested by the Committee
To give you the deed conveying the monument to your
care,
With the feu-charter of the ground, therefore, sir, I'd have
you beware."

Then the Chief Magistrate Forbes to Lord Breadalbane
said,
"My noble Lord, I accept the charge, and you needn't be
afraid.
Really it gives me much pleasure in accepting as I now do
from thee
This Memorial, along with the deeds, on behalf of
Aberfeldy."

Then Major Menzies proposed three cheers for the burgh
of Aberfeldy,
And three cheers were given right heartily.
Then the Taymouth Band played "God Save the Queen,"
Then the processionists marched to the New Public School,
happy and serene.

Then there was a banquet held in the school,
At which three hundred sat down and ate till they were
full;
And Lord Breadalbane presided, and had on his right,
Magistrates, Colonels, and Provosts, a most beautiful sight.

And the toasts of "The Queen," "Prince and Princess of
Wales," were given,
Wishing them prosperity while they are living;

Then the noble Chairman proposed "The Army, Navy
and Volunteers,"
Which was loudly responded to with three loud cheers.

Then Colonel Smith, of the Highland Volunteers, from
Bonnie Dundee,
Replied for the Volunteers right manfully.
Then the noble Chairman said, "The toast I have now to
propose
Is long life and prosperity to the Royal Highlanders in
spite of their foes."

Then the toast was drunk with Highland honours and
hearts so true,
While Pipe-Major M'Dougall played "The 42nd March at
Waterloo."
So ended the proceedings in honour of the Black Watch,
the bravest of men,
And the company with one accord sung the National
Anthem.

AN ADDRESS TO THE REV. GEORGE GILFILLAN

All hail to the Rev. George Gilfillan of Dundee,
He is the greatest preacher I did ever hear or see.
He is a man of genius bright,
And in him his congregration does delight,
Because they find him to be honest and plain,
Affable in temper, and seldom known to complain.
He preaches in a plain straightforward way,
The people flock to hear him night and day,
And hundreds from the doors are often turn'd away,
Because he is the greatest preacher of the present day.
He has written the life of Sir Walter Scott,
And while he lives he will never be forgot,
Nor when he is dead,
Because by his admirers it will be often read;
And fill their minds with wonder and delight,

And wile away the tedious hours on a cold winter's night.
He has also written about the Bards of the Bible,
Which occupied nearly three years in which he was not
    idle,
Because when he sits down to write he does it with might
    and main,
And to get an interview with him it would be almost vain,
And in that he is always right,
Do it with all your might.
Rev. George Gilfillan of Dundee, I must conclude my muse,
And to write in praise of thee my pen does not refuse,
For the Bible tells us whatever your hands findeth to do,
Nor does it give me pain to tell the world fearlessly, that
    when
You are dead they shall not look upon your like again.

AN ADDRESS TO SHAKESPEARE

Immortal! William Shakespeare, there's none can you
    excel,
You have drawn out your characters remarkably well,
Which is delightful for to see enacted upon the stage—
For instance, the love-sick Romeo, or Othello, in a rage;
His writings are a treasure, which the world cannot repay,
He was the greatest poet of the past or of the present day—
Also the greatest dramatist, and is worthy of the name,
I'm afraid the world shall never look upon his like again.
His tragedy of Hamlet is moral and sublime,
And for purity of language, nothing can be more fine—
For instance, to hear the fair Ophelia making her moan,
At her father's grave, sad and alone. . . .
In his beautiful play, "As You Like It," one passage is very
    fine,
Just for instance in the forest of Arden, the language is
    sublime,
Where Orlando speaks of his Rosalind, most lovely and
    divine,

And no other poet I am sure has written anything more
   fine;
His language is spoken in the Church and by the Advocate
   at the bar,
Here and there and everywhere throughout the world afar;
His writings abound with gospel truths, moral and sublime,
And I'm sure in my opinion they are surpassing fine;
In his beautiful tragedy of Othello, one passage is very fine,
Just for instance where Cassio looses his lieutenancy
. . . By drinking too much wine;
And in grief he exclaim, "Oh! that men should put an
Enemy in their mouths to steal away their brains."
In his great tragedy of Richard the III, one passage is very
   fine
Where the Duchess of York invokes the aid of the Divine
For to protect her innocent babes from the murderer's
   uplifted hand,
And smite him powerless, and save her babes, I'm sure 'tis
   really grand.
Immortal! Bard of Avon, your writings are divine,
And will live in the memories of your admirers until the
   end of time;
Your plays are read in family circles with wonder and
   delight,
While seated around the fireside on a cold winter's night.

THE QUEEN'S DIAMOND JUBILEE
CELEBRATIONS

'Twas in the year of 1897, and on the 22nd of June,
Her Majesty's Diamond Jubilee in London caused a great
   boom;
Because high and low came from afar to see,
The grand celebrations at Her Majesty's Diamond Jubilee.
People were there from almost every foreign land,
Which made the scene really imposing and grand;
Especially the Queen's carriage, drawn by eight cream-
   coloured bays,

And when the spectators saw it joyous shouts they did
    raise.

Oh! it was a most gorgeous sight to be seen,
Numerous foreign magnates were there for to see the
    Queen;
And to the vast multitude there of women and men,
Her Majesty for two hours showed herself to them.

The head of the procession looked very grand—
A party of the Horse Guards with their gold-belaced band;
Which also headed the procession of the Colonial States,
While slowly they rode on until opposite the Palace gates.

Then the sound of the National Anthem was heard quite
    clear,
And the sound the hearts of the mighty crowd it did cheer;
As they heard the loyal hymning on the morning air,
The scene was most beautiful and surpassing fair.

On the house tops thousands of people were to be seen,
All in eager expectation of seeing the Queen;
And all of them seemed to be happy and gay,
Which enhanced the scene during the day.

And when Field Marshal Roberts in the procession passed
    by,
The cheers from thousands of people arose very high;
And to see him on his war horse was inspiring to see,
Because he rode his charger most splendidly.
The Natal mounted troops were loudly cheered, they looked
    so grand,
And also the London Irish Emerald Isle Band;
Oh it was a most magnificent sight to see.
The Malta Militia and Artillery,
And the Trinidad Artillery, and also bodies of infantry,
And, as the crowd gazed theron, it filled their hearts with
    glee.
Her Majesty looked well considering her years,

And from the vast crowd burst forth joyous cheers;
And Her Majesty bowed to the shouts of acclamation,
And smiled upon the crowd with a loving look of admiration.

His Excellency Chan Yin Hun in his carriage was a great
attraction,
And his Oriental garb seemed to give the people great
satisfaction;
While the two little Battenberg's carriage, as it drove along,
Received from the people cheering loud and long.

And when the Dragoon Guards and the Hussars filed past
at the walk,
Then loudly in their praise the people did talk;
And the cavalry took forty minutes to trot past,
While the spectators in silent wonder stood aghast.

Her Majesty the Empress Frederick a great sensation made,
She was one of the chief attractions in the whole cavalcade;
And in her carriage was the Princess Louise, the Marchioness of Lorne,
In a beautiful white dress, which did her person adorn.
The scene in Piccadilly caused a great sensation,
The grand decorations there were the theme of admiration;
And the people in St. James Street were taken by surprise,
Because the lovely decorations dazzled their eyes.

The 42nd Highlanders looked very fine,
When they appeared and took up a position on the line;
And the magnificent decorations in the Strand,
As far east as the Griffin was attractive and grand.

And the grandstand from Buckingham Palace to Temple
Bar,
Was crowded with eager eyes from afar,
Looking on the floral decorations and flags unfurled,
Which has been the grandest spectacle ever seen in the
world.

The corner building of St. James Street side was lovely to
   view,
Ornamented with pink and white bunting and a screen of
   blue;
And to the eye, the inscription thereon most beautiful
   seems :
"Thou art alone the Queen of earthly Queens."

The welcome given to Commander-in-Chief Lord Wolseley
   was very flattering,
The people cheered him until the streets did ring;
And the foreign princess were watched with rivetted
   admiration,
And caused among the sight-seers great consternation.
And private householders seemed to vie with each other,
In the lavishness of their decorations, and considered it no
   bother;
And never before in the memory of man,
Has there been a national celebration so grand.

And in conclusion, I most earnestly do pray,
May God protect Her Majesty for many a day;
My blessing on her noble form and on her lofty head,
And may she wear a crown of glory hereafter when dead.

THE DEATH OF THE QUEEN

Alas! our noble and generous Queen Victoria is dead,
And I hope her soul to Heaven has fled,
To sing and rejoice with saints above,
Where all is joy, peace, and love.

'Twas on January 22, 1901, in the evening she died at 6.30
   o'clock,
Which to the civilised world has been a great shock;
She was surrounded by her children and grandchildren
   dear,
And for the motherly, pious Queen they shed many a tear.

She has been a model and faithful Queen,
Very few like her have been;
She has acted virtuously during her long reign,
And I'm afraid the world will never see her like again.

And during her reign she was beloved by the high and the
    low,
And through her decease the people's hearts are full of woe,
Because she was kind to her subjects at home and abroad,
And now she's receiving her reward from the Eternal God.

And during her reign in this world of trouble and strife
Several attempts were made to take her life;
Maclean he tried to shoot her, but he did fail,
But he was arrested and sent to an asylum, which made him
    bewail.

Victoria was a noble Queen, the people must confess,
She was most charitable to them while in distress;
And in her disposition she wasn't proud nor vain,
And tears for her loss will fall as plentiful as rain.

The people around Balmoral will shed many tears
Owing to her visits amongst them for many years;
She was very kind to the old, infirm women there,
By giving them provisions and occasionally a prayer.

And while at Balmoral she found work for men
    unemployed,
Which made the hearts of the poor men feel overjoyed;
And for Her Majesty they would have laid down their lives,
Because sometimes she saved them from starving, and their
    Wives.

Many happy days she spent at Balmoral,
Viewing the blooming heather and the bonnie Highland
    floral,
Along with Prince Albert, her husband dear,
But alas! when he died she shed many a tear.

She was very charitable, as everybody knows,
But the loss of her husband caused her many woes,
Because he cheered her at Balmoral as they the heather
  trod,
But I hope she has met him now at the Throne of God.

They ascended the Hill of Morven when she was in her
  fortieth year,
And Her Majesty was delighted as she viewed the Highland
  deer;
Also dark Lochnagar, which is most beautiful to see,
Not far from Balmoral and the dark River Dee.

I hope they are walking in Heaven together as they did in
  life,
In the beautiful celestial regions, free from all strife,
Where God's family together continually meet,
Where the streets are paved with gold, and everything
  complete.

Alas! for the loss of Queen Victoria the people will mourn,
But she unto them can never return;
Therefore to mourn for her is all in vain,
Knowing that she can never return again.

Therefore, good people, one and all,
Let us be prepared for death when God does on us call,
Like the good and noble Queen Victoria of renown,
The greatest and most virtuous Queen that ever wore a
  crown.

NORA, THE MAID OF KILLARNEY

Down by the beautiful Lakes of Killarney,
Oft times I have met my own dear Barney,
In the sweet summer time of the year,
In the silvery moonlight so clear,

I've rambled with my sweetheart Barney,
Along the green banks of the Lakes of Killarney.

The Lakes of Killarney are most lovely to be seen
In the summer season when nature's face is green,
Especially in the beautiful silvery moonlight,
When its waters do shine like silver bright;
Such was the time when me and my Barney
Went to walk by the purty Lakes of Killarney.

My Barney was beautiful, gallant, and gay,
But, alas, he has left me and gone far away,
To that foreign country called Amerikay;
But when he returns we will get married without delay,
And again we will roam by the Lakes of Killarney,
Me and my sweetheart, charming Barney.

And until he returns I will feel rather sad,
For while walking with Barney I always felt glad;
May God send him home again safe to me,
And he will fill my sad heart with glee,
While we walk by the Lakes of Killarney.

I dreamt one night I was walking with Barney,
Down by the beautiful Lakes of Killarney,
And he he said, "Nora, dear Nora, don't fret for me,
For I will soon come home to thee;
And I will build a nice cabin near the Lakes of Killarney,
And Nora will live happy with her own dear Barney."

But, alas, I awoke from my beautiful dream,
For, och, it was a most lovely scene;
But I hope it will happen some unexpected day,
When Barney comes home from Amerikay;
Then Barney will relate his adventures to me,
As we walk by the silvery Lakes of Killarney.

We will ramble among its green trees and green bushes,
And hear the sweet songs of the blackbirds and thrushes,

And gaze on its lovely banks so green,
And its waters glittering like crystal in the moonlight's
   sheen;
Och! how I long to be walking with Barney,
Along the green banks of the Lakes of Killarney.

Of all the spots in Ireland, Killarney for me,
For 'twas there I first met my dear Barney:
He was singing, I remember, right merrily;
And his singing filled my heart with glee,
And he said, "Nora, dear Nora, will you walk with me,
For you are the prettiest girl I ever did see."

"Now, Barney," I said, "you are just mocking me,
When you say no other girl like me you can see";
Then he said, "Nora, you are the only girl I do love,
And this I do swear by the saints above,
I will marry you, dear Nora, without delay,
When I come home from Amerikay."

But when Barney landed in Amerikay,
He courted another girl without dismay,
And he married her in the month of May,
And when I heard it I fainted away;
So maidens beware of such men as Barney,
Or else they will deceive ye with their flattering blarney.

THE LITTLE MATCH GIRL

It was biting cold, and the falling snow,
Which filled a poor little match girl's heart with woe,
Who was bareheaded and barefooted, as she went along the
   street,
Crying, 'Who'll buy my matches? for I want pennies to
   buy some meat!"

When she left home she had slippers on;
But, alas! poor child, now they were gone.
For she lost both of them while hurrying across the street,
Out of the way of two carriages which were near by her
        feet.

So the little girl went on, while the snow fell thick and fast;
And the child's heart felt cold and downcast,
For nobody had bought any matches that day,
Which filled her little mind with grief and dismay.

Alas! she was hungry and shivering with cold;
So in a corner between two houses she made bold
To take shelter from the violent storm.
Poor little waif! wishing to herself she'd never been born.

And she grew colder and colder, and feared to go home
For fear of her father beating her; and she felt woe-begone
Because she could carry home no pennies to buy bread,
And to go home without pennies she was in dread.

The large flakes of snow covered her ringlets of fair hair;
While the passers-by for her had no care,
As they hurried along to their homes at a quick pace,
While the cold wind blew in the match girl's face.

As night wore on her hands were numb with cold,
And no longer her strength could her uphold,
When an idea into her little head came:
She'd strike a match and warm her hands at the flame.

And she lighted the match, and it burned brightly,
And it helped to fill her heart with glee;
And she thought she was sitting at a stove very grand;
But, alas! she was found dead, with a match in her hand!

Her body was found half-covered with snow,
And as the people gazed thereon their hearts were full of
        woe;

117

And many present let fall a burning tear
Because she was found dead on the last night of the year,

In that mighty city of London, wherein is plenty of gold—
But, alas; their charity towards street waifs is rather cold.
But I hope the match girl's in Heaven, beside her Saviour
    dear,
A bright reward for all the hardships she suffered here.

BEAUTIFUL COMRIE

AND ITS SURROUNDINGS

Ye lovers of the picturesque, away, away!
To beautiful Comrie and have a holiday;
And bask in the sunshine and inhale the fragrant air
Emanating from the woodlands and shrubberies there.

The charming village of Comrie is most lovely to be seen,
Especially in the summer season when the trees are green;
And near by is Loch Earn and its waters sparkling clear,
And as the tourist gazes thereon his spirits it will cheer.

Then St. Fillans is a beautiful spot, I must confess,
It is really a picture of rural loveliness;
Because out of the quiet lake the river ripples merrily,
And all round are hills beautiful in shape and nothing
    uncomely.

The rocky knoll to the south is a most seductive place,
And in the hotel there visitors will find every solace;
And the flower-decked cottages are charming to see,
Also handsome villas suitable for visitors of high and low
    degree.

Then there's St. Fillan's Hill, a prehistoric fort,
And visitors while there to it should resort;

And to the tourist the best approach is from the west,
Because in climbing the hill his strength it will test.
And descending the hill as best one may,
The scene makes the tourist's heart feel gay;
And by the west side is reached a wooded dell,
And about two hundred yards from that there's St. Fillan's
    Well.

Oh, charming Comrie! I must conclude my lay,
And to write in praise of thee I virtually do say
That your lovely mountains and silver birches will drive
    dull care away:
Therefore lovers of the picturesque, away, away!

To beautiful Comrie and have a holiday,
And I'm sure you will return with spirits light and gay,
After viewing the Sylvan beauties and hoary beeches there,
Also pines, ferns, and beautiful oaks, I do declare.

BEAUTIFUL BALMORAL

Ye lovers of the picturesque, away and see
Beautiful Balmoral, near by the River Dee;
There ye will see the deer browsing on the heathery hills,
While adown their sides run clear sparkling rills.

Which the traveller can drink of when he feels dry,
And admire the dark River Dee near by,
Rolling smoothly and silently on its way,
Which is most lovely to see on a summer day.

There the trout do sport and play
During the live-long summer day;
Also plenty of salmon are there to be seen,
Glittering like silver in the sun's sheen.

And the mountains are rugged and wild to be seen,
But the woodlands are beautiful when Nature's face is
green;
There numerous rabbits do gambol all day
Amongst the green shrubbery all lively and gay.

There's one charming spot most magnificent to be seen,
'Tis Balmoral Castle, the Highland Home of our Queen;
The surrounding scenery is enchanting to see,
While near by rolls past the lovely River Dee.

Therefore, ye lovers of the picturesque, away and see
Beautiful Balmoral Castle and its grand scenery,
And the sight will fill your hearts with glee,
As ye walk along the bonnie banks o' the River Dee.

BEAUTIFUL TORQUAY

All ye lovers of the picturesque, away
To beautiful Torquay and spend a holiday;
'Tis health for invalids for to go there
To view the beautiful scenery and inhale the fragrant air,
Especially in the winter and spring-time of the year,
When the weather is not too hot, but is balmy and clear.

Torquay lies in a very deep and well-sheltered spot,
And at first sight by strangers it won't be forgot;
'Tis said to be the mildest place in all England,
And surrounded by lofty hills most beautiful and grand.

'Twas here that William of Orange first touched English
ground,
And as he viewed the beautiful spot his heart with joy did
rebound;
And an obelisk marks the spot where he did stand,
And which for long will be remembered throughout
England.

Torquay, with its pier and its diadem of white,
Is a most beautiful and very dazzling sight,
With its white villas glittering on the sides of its green hills,
And as the tourist gazes thereon with joy his heart fills.

The heights around Torquay are most beautiful to be seen,
Especially when the trees and shrubberies are green,
And to see the pretty houses under the cliff is a treat,
And the little town enclosed where two deep valleys meet.

There is also a fine bathing establishment near the pier,
Where the tourist can bathe without any fear;
And as the tourists there together doth stroll,
I advise them to visit a deep chasm called Daddy's Hole.

Then there's Bablicome, only two miles from Torquay,
Which makes the stranger's heart feel gay,
As he stands on the cliff four hundred feet above the sea,
Looking down, 'tis sure to fill his heart with ecstasy.

The lodging-houses at Bablicome are magnificent to be seen,
And the accommodation there would suit either king or
    queen,
And there's some exquisite cottages embowered in the
    woodland,
And sloping down to the sea shore, is really very grand.

You do not wonder at Napoleon's exclamation
As he stood on the deck of the "Bellepheron," in a fit of
    admiration,
When the vessel was lying to windbound,
He exclaimed—"Oh, what a beautiful country!" his joy
    was profound.

And as the tourist there in search of beautiful spots doth
    rove,
Let us not forget to enquire for Anstey's Cove,
And there they will see a beautiful beach of milky white,
And the sight will fill their hearts with delight.

Oh! beautiful Torquay, with your lovely scenery,
And your magnificent cottages sloping down to the sea,
You are the most charming spot in all England,
With you picturesque bay and villas most grand.

And, in conclusion, to tourists I will say,
Off! off to Torquay and make no delay,
For the scenery is magnificent, and salubrious the air,
And 'tis good for the health to reside there.

THE ANCIENT TOWN OF LEITH

Ancient town of Leith, most wonderful to be seen,
With your many handsome buildings, and lovely links so
    green,
And the first buildings I may mention are the Courthouse
    and Town Hall,
Also Trinity House, and the Sailors' Home of Call.

Then as for Leith Fort, it was erected in 1779, which is
    really grand,
And which now is the artillery headquarters in Bonnie
    Scotland;
And as for the Docks, they are magnificent to see,
They comprise five docks, two piers, 1,141 yards long
    respectively.
And there's steamboat communication with London and the
    North of Scotland,
And the fares are really cheap and the accommodation
    most grand;
Then there's many public works in Leith, such as flour
    mills,
And chemical works, where medicines are made for curing
    many ills.

Besides, there are sugar refineries and distilleries,
Also engineer works, saw-mills, rope-works, and breweries,

Where many of the inhabitants are daily employed,
And the wages they receive make their hearts feel over-
joyed.

In past times Leith shared the fortunes of Edinboro',
Because it withstood nine months' siege, which caused them
great sorrow;
They fought against the Protestants in 1559 and in '60,
But they beat them back manfully and made them flee.

Then there's Bailie Gibson's food shop, most elegant to be
seen,
And the fish he sells there are beautiful and clean;
And for himself, he is a very good man,
And to deny it there's few people can.

The suburban villas of Leith are elegant and grand,
With accommodation that might suit the greatest lady in
the land;
And the air is pure and good for the people's health,—
And health, I'm sure, is better by far than wealth.

The Links of Leith are beautiful for golfers to play,
After they have finished the toils of the day;
It is good for their health to play at golf there,
Or that very beautiful green, and breathe the pure air.

The old town of Leith is situated at the junction of the
River of Leith,
Which springs from the land of heather and heath;
And no part in the Empire is growing so rapidly,
Which the inhabitants of Leith are right glad to see.

And Leith in every way is in itself independent,
And has been too busy to attend to its own adornment;
But I venture to say and also mention
That the authorities to the town will pay more attention.

Ancient town of Leith, I must now conclude my muse,
And to write in praise of thee my pen does not refuse,
Because the inhabitants to me have been very kind,
And I'm sure more generous people would be hard to find.

They are very affable in temper and void of pride,
And I hope God will always for them provide;
May He shower his blessings upon them land and sea,
Because they have always been very kind to me.

THE CITY OF PERTH

BEAUTIFUL Ancient City of Perth,
One of the fairest on the earth,
With your stately mansions and scenery most fine,
Which seems very beautiful in the summer time;
And the beautiful silvery Tay,
Rolling smoothly on its way,
And glittering like silver in the sunshine—
And the Railway Bridge across it is really sublime.
The scenery is very beautiful when in full bloom,
It far excels the river Doon—
For the North Inch and South Inch is most beautiful to
    behold,
Where the buttercups do shine in the sunshine like gold.

And there's the Palace of Scone, most beautiful to be seen,
Near by the river Tay and the North Inch so green,
Whereon is erected the statue of Prince Albert, late husband
    of the Queen,
And also the statue of Sir Walter Scott is most beautiful to
    be seen,
Erected on the South Inch, which would please the Queen,
And recall to her memory his novels she has read—
And cause her to feel a pang for him that is dead.

Beautiful City of Perth, along the river Tay, I must con-
    clude my lay,
And to write in praise of thee my heart does not gainsay,
To tell the world fearlessly, without the least dismay—
With your stately mansions and the beautiful river Tay,
You're one of the fairest Cities of the present day.

BONNIE DUNDEE IN 1878

Oh, Bonnie Dundee, I will sing in thy praise
A few but true simple lays,
Regarding some of your beauties of the present day—
And virtually speaking, there's none can them gainsay;
There's no other town I know of with you can compare
For spinning mills and lassies fair,
And for stately buildings there's none can excel
The beautiful Albert Institute or the Queen's Hotel,
For it is most handsome to be seen,
Where accommodation can be had for Duke, Lord or
    Queen,
And the four pillars of the front are made of Aberdeen
    granite, very fine,
And most beautiful does shine, just like a looking glass,
And for beauty and grandeur there's none can them surpass
And your fine shops in Reform Street,
Very few can with them compete
For superfine goods, there's none can excel,
From Inverness to Clerkenwell.
And your Tramways, I must confess,
That they have proved a complete success,
Which I am right glad to see . . .
And a very great improvement to Bonnie Dundee.
And there's the Royal Arch, most handsome to be seen,
Erected to the memory of our most Gracious Queen—
Most magnificent to see,
And a very great honour to the people of Dundee.

125

Then there's the Baxter Park, most beautiful to see,
And a great boon it is to the people of Dundee,
For there they can enjoy themselves when they are free
    from care,
By inhaling the perfumed air,
Emanating from the sweet flowers and green trees and
    shrubs there.
Oh, Bonnie Dundee! I must conclude my muse,
And to write in praise of thee, my pen does not refuse,
Your beauties that I have alluded to are most worthy to
    see,
And in conclusion, I will call thee Bonnie Dundee!

LOCH NESS

BEAUTIFUL Loch Ness,
The truth to express,
Your landscapes are lovely and gay,
Along each side of your waters, to Fort Augustus all the
    way,
Your scenery is romantic . . .
With rocks and hills gigantic . . .
Enough to make one frantic,
As they view thy beautiful heathery hills,
And their clear crystal rills,
And the beautiful woodlands so green,
On a fine summer day . . .
From Inverness all the way . . .
Where the deer and the roe together doth play;
And the beautiful Falls of Foyers with its crystal spray,
As clear as the day,
Enchanting and gay,
To the traveller as he gazes thereon,
That he feels amazed with delight,
To see the water falling from such a height,
That his head feels giddy with the scene,
As he views the Falls of Foyers and the woodlands so green,

126

That he exclaims in an ecstasy of delight—
Oh, beautiful Loch Ness!
I must sincerely confess,
That you are the most beautiful to behold,
With your lovely landscapes and water so cold.
And as he turns from the scene, he says with a sigh—
Oh, beautiful Loch Ness! I must bid you good-bye.

A DESCRIPTIVE POEM ON
THE SILVERY TAY

Beautiful silvery Tay,
With your landscapes, so lovely and gay,
Along each side of your waters, to Perth all the way;
No other river in the world has got scenery more fine,
Only I am told the beautiful Rhine,
Near to Wormit Bay, it seems very fine,
Where the Railway Bridge is towering above its waters
        sublime,
And the beautiful ship Mars,
With her Juvenile Tars,
Both lively and gay,
Does carelessly lie
By night and by day,
In the beautiful Bay
Of the silvery Tay.
Beautiful, beautiful! silvery Tay,
Thy scenery is enchanting on a fine summer day,
Near by Balmerino it is beautiful to behold,
When the trees are in full bloom and the cornfields seem
        like gold—
And nature's face seems gay,
And the lambkins they do play,
And the humming bee is on the wing,
It is enough to make one sing,
While they carelessly do stray,
Along the beautiful banks of the silvery Tay,
Beautiful silvery Tay, rolling smoothly on your way,

Near by Newport, as clear as the day,
Thy scenery around is charming I'll be bound . . .
And would make the heart of any one feel light and gay on
    a fine summer day.
To view the beautiful scenery along the banks of the silvery
    Tay.

THE BONNIE LASS O' DUNDEE

O' a' the toons that I've been in,
   I dearly love Dundee,
It's there the bonnie lassie lives,
   The lass I love to see.
Her face is fair, broon is her hair,
   And dark blue is her e'e,
And aboon a' the lasses 'er I saw,
   There's nane like her to me—
The bonnie broon-hair'd lassie o' Bonnie Dundee.

I see her in my night dreams,
   Wi' her bonnie blue e'e,
And her face it is the fairest,
   That ever I did see;
And aboon a' the lassies e'er I saw,
   There's nane like her to me,
For she makes my heart feel lichtsome,
   And I'm aye right glad to see—
The bonnie broon-hair'd lassie o' Bonnie Dundee.

Her eyes, they beam with innocence,
   Most lovely for to see,
And her heart it is as free from guile,
   As a child on its mothers' knee;
And aboon a' the lassies e'er I saw,
   There's nane like her to me,
For she aye seems so happy,
   And has a blythe blink in her e'e—
The bonnie broon-hair'd lassie o' Bonnie Dundee.

The lassie is tidy in her claes,
   Baith neat and clean to see;
And her body's sma and slender,
   And a neat foot has she;
And aboon a' the lassies e'er I saw,
   There's nane like her to me—
The bonnie broon-hair'd lassie o' Bonnie Dundee.

She sings like the nightingale,
   Richt merrily, or a wee lintie,
Wi' its heart fou' o' glee,
   And she's frisky as a bee;
And aboon a' the lassies e'er I saw,
   There's nane like her to me—
The bonnie broon-hair'd lassie o' Bonnie Dundee.

The lassie is as handsome
   As the lily on the lea,
And her mou' it is as red
   As a cherry on a tree;
And she's a' the world to me,
   The bonnie broon-hair'd lassie
With the bonnie blue e'e.
   She's the joy o' my heart
And the flower o' Dundee.

LINES IN PRAISE OF TOMMY ATKINS

Success to Tommy Atkins, he's a very brave man,
And to deny it there's few people can;
And to face his foreign foes he's never afraid,
Therefore he's not a beggar, as Rudyard Kipling has said.

No, he's paid by our Government, and is worthy of his
   hire;
And from our shores in time of war he makes our foes
   retire,

He doesn't need to beg; no, nothing so low;
No, he considers it more honourable to face a foreign foe.

No, he's not a beggar, he's a more useful man,
And, as Shakespeare has said, his life's but a span;
And at the cannon's mouth he seeks for reputation,
He doesn't go from door to door seeking a donation.

Oh, think of Tommy Atkins when from home far away,
Lying on the battlefield, earth's cold clay;
And a stone or his knapsack pillowing his head,
And his comrades lying near by him wounded and dead.

And while lying there, poor fellow, he thinks of his wife at
       home,
And his heart bleeds at the thought, and he does moan;
And down his cheek flows many a silent tear,
When he thinks of his friends and children dear.

Kind Christians, think of him when far, far away,
Fighting for his Queen and Country without dismay;
May God protect him wherever he goes,
And give him strength to conquer his foes.

To call a soldier a beggar is a very degrading name,
And in my opinion it's a very great shame;
And the man that calls him a beggar is not the soldier's
       friend,
And no sensible soldier should on him depend.

A soldier is a man that ought to be respected,
And by his country shouldn't be neglected;
For he fights our foreign foes, and in danger of his life,
Leaving behind him relatives and his dear wife.

Then hurrah for Tommy Atkins, he's the people's friend,
Because when foreign foes assail us he does us defend;
He is not a beggar, as Rudyard Kipling has said,
No, he doesn't need to beg, he lives by his trade.

And in conclusion I will say,
Don't forget his wife and children when he's far away;
But try and help them all you can,
For remember Tommy Atkins is a very useful man.

THE RELIEF OF MAFEKING

SUCCESS to Colonel Baden-Powell and his praises loudly
    sing,
For being so brave in relieving Mafeking,
With his gallant little band of eight hundred men,
They made the Boers fly from Mafeking like sheep escaping
    from a pen.

'Twas in the year of 1900 and on the 18th of May,
That Colonel Baden-Powell beat the Boers without dismay,
And made them fly from Mafeking without delay,
Which will be handed down to posterity for many a day.

Colonel Baden-Powell is a very brave man,
And to deny it, I venture to say, few men can;
He is a noble hero be it said,
For at the siege of Mafeking he never was afraid.

And during the siege Colonel Baden was cheerful and gay,
While the starving population were living on brawn each
    day;
And alas! the sufferings of the women and children were
    great,
Yet they all submitted patiently to their fate.

For seven months besieged they fought the Boers without
    dismay,
Until at last the Boers were glad to run away;
Because Baden-Powell's gallant band had put them to flight
By cannon shot and volleys of musketry to the left and
    right.

Then long live Baden-Powell and his brave little band,
For during the siege of Mafeking they made a bold stand
Against yelling thousands of Boers who were thirsting for
    their blood,
But as firm as a rock against them they fearlessly stood.

Oh! think of them living on brawn extracted from horse
    hides,
While the inhuman Boers their sufferings deride,
Knowing that the women's hearts with grief were torn
As they looked on their children's faces that looked sad and
    forlorn.

For 217 days the Boers tried to obtain Mafeking's surrender,
But their strategy was futile owing to its noble defender,
Colonel Baden-Powell, that hero of renown,
Who, by his masterly generalship, saved the town.

Methinks I see him and his gallant band,
Looking terror to the foe : Oh! The sight was really grand,
As he cried, "Give it to them, lads; let's do or die;
And from Mafeking we'll soon make them fly,
And we'll make them rue their rash undertaking
The day they laid siege to the town of Mafeking."

Long life and prosperity to Colonel Baden-Powell,
For there's very few generals can him excel;
And he is now the Hero of Mafeking, be it told,
And his name should be engraved on medals of gold.

I wish him and his gallant little band every success,
For relieving the people of Mafeking while in distress;
They made the Boers rue their rash undertaking
The day they laid siege to the town of Mafeking.

For during the defence of Mafeking
From grief he kept the people's hearts from breaking,
Because he sang to them and did recite
Passages from Shakespeare which did their hearts delight.

THE BATTLE OF GLENCOE

'Twas in the month of October, and in the year of 1899,
Which the Boers will remember for a very long time,
Because by the British Army they received a crushing blow;
And were driven from Smith's Hill at the Battle of Glencoe.

The Boers' plan of the battle was devised with great skill,
And about 7000 men of them were camped on Smith's Hill;
And at half-past five the battle began,
As the Boers behaved bravely to a man.

At twenty minutes to six two of the British batteries
    opened fire,
And early in the fight some of the Boers began to retire;
And in half an hour the Boers' artillery had ceased to fire,
And from the crest of the hill they began to retire.

And General Symons with his staff was watching every
    detail,
The brave hero whose courage in the battle didn't fail;
Because he ordered the King's Royal Rifles and the Dublin
    Fusiliers,
To advance in skirmishing order, which they did with three
    cheers.

Then they boldly advanced in very grand style,
And encouraged by their leaders all the while;
And their marching in skirmishing order was beautiful to
    see,
As they advanced boldly to attack the enemy.

For over an hour the advance continued without dismay,
Until they had to take a breath by the way;
They felt so fatigued climbing up Smith's Hill,
But, nevertheless, the brave heroes did it with a will.

Then they prepared to attack the enemy,
And with wild battle-cries they attacked them vigorously;

And with one determined rush they ascended the hill,
And drove the Boers from their position sore against their
    will.

But, alas, General Symons received a mortal wound,
Which caused his soldiers' sorrow to be profound;
But still they fought on manfully without any dread;
But, alas, brave General Symons now is dead.

Oh! It was a most inspiring and a magnificent sight,
To see the Hussars spurring their steeds with all their might;
And charging the Boers with their lances of steel,
Which hurled them from their saddles and made them reel.

The battle raged for six hours and more,
While British cannon Smith's Hill up tore;
Still the Boers fought manfully, without dismay,
But in a short time they had to give way.

For the Gordon Highlanders soon put an end to the fight,
Oh! it was a most gorgeous and thrilling sight,
To see them with their bagpipes playing, and one ringing
    cheer,
And from Smith's Hill they soon did the Boers clear.

And at the charge of the bayonet they made them fly,
While their leaders cried, "Forward, my lads, do or die,"
And the Boers' blood copiously they did spill,
And the Boers were forced to fly from Smith's Hill.

And in conclusion I hope and pray
The British will be successful when from home far away;
And long may the Gordons be able to conquer the foe,
At home or abroad, wherever they go.

THE BATTLE OF WATERLOO

'Twas in the year 1815, and on the 18th day of June,
That British cannon, against the French army, loudly did
    boom,
Upon the ever memorable bloody field of Waterloo;
Which Napoleon remembered while in St. Helena, and
    bitterly did rue.

The morning of the 18th was gloomy and cheerless to
    behold,
But the British soon recovered from the severe cold
That they had endured the previous rainy night;
And each man prepared to burnish his arms for the coming
    fight.

Then the morning passed in mutual arrangements for
    battle,
And the French guns, at half-past eleven, loudly did rattle;
And immediately the order for attack was given,
Then the bullets flew like lightning till the Heaven's seemed
    riven.
The place from which Bonaparte viewed the bloody field
Was the farmhouse of La Belle Alliance, which some pro-
    tection did yield;
And there he remained for the most part of the day,
Pacing to and fro with his hands behind him in doubtful
    dismay.

The Duke of Wellington stood upon a bridge behind La
    Haye,
And viewed the British army in all their grand array,
And where danger threatened most the noble Duke was
    found
In the midst of shot and shell on every side around.

Hougemont was the key of the Duke of Wellington's
    position,
A spot that was naturally very strong, and a great
    acquisition

To the Duke and his staff during the day,
Which the Coldstream Guards held to the last, without
dismay.

The French 2nd Corps were principally directed during the
day
To carry Hougemont farmhouse without delay;
So the farmhouse in quick succession they did attack,
But the British guns on the heights above soon drove them
back.

But still the heavy shot and shells ploughed through the
walls;
Yet the brave guards resolved to hold the place no matter
what befalls;
And they fought manfully to the last, with courage un-
shaken,
Until the tower of Hougemont was in a blaze but still it
remained untaken.

By these desperate attacks Napoleon lost ten thousand men,
And left them weltering in their gore like sheep in a pen;
And the British lost one thousand men—which wasn't very
great,
Because the great Napoleon met with a crushing defeat.

The advance of Napoleon on the right was really very fine,
Which was followed by a general onset upon the British
line,
In which three hundred pieces of artillery opened their
cannonade;
But the British artillery played upon them, and great
courage displayed.

For ten long hours it was a continued succession of attacks;
Whilst the British cavalry charged them in all their draw-
backs;
And the courage of the British Army was great in square at
Waterloo,

Because hour after hour they were mowed down in numbers not a few.

At times the temper of the troops had very nearly failed,
Especially amongst the Irish regiments who angry railed;
And they cried: "When will we get at them? Show us the way
That we may avenge the death of our comrades without delay?"

But "be steady and cool, my brave lads," was their officers' command,
While each man was ready to charge with gun in hand;
Oh, Heaven! it was pitiful to see their comrades lying around,
Dead and weltering in their gore, and cumbering the ground.

It was a most dreadful sight to behold,
Heaps upon heaps of dead men lying stiff and cold;
While the cries of the dying was lamentable to hear;
And for the loss of their comrades many a soldier shed a tear.

Men and horses fell on every side around,
Whilst heavy cannon shot tore up the ground;
And musket balls in thousands flew,
And innocent blood bedewed the field of Waterloo.

Methinks I see the solid British square,
Whilst the shout of the French did rend the air,
As they rush against the square of steel.
Which forced them back and made them reel.

And when a gap was made in that square,
The cry of "Close up! Close up!" did rend the air,
"And charge them with your bayonets, and make them fly!
And Scotland for ever! be the cry."

The French and British closed in solid square,
While the smoke of the heavy cannonade darkened the air;
Then the noble Picton deployed his division into line,
And drove back the enemy in a very short time.

Then Lord Anglesey seized on the moment, and charging
with the Greys,
Whilst the Inniskillings burst through everything, which
they did always;
Then the French infantry fell in hundreds by the swords of
the Dragoons;
Whilst the thundering of the cannonade loudly booms.

And the Eagles of the 45th and 105th were all captured that
day,
And upwards of 2000 prisoners, all in grand array;
But, alas! at the head of his division, the noble Picton fell,
While the Highlanders played a lament for him they loved
so well.

Then the French cavalry receded from the square they
couldn't penetrate,
Still Napoleon thought to weary the British into defeat;
But when he saw his columns driven back in dismay,
He cried, "How beautifully these English fight, but they
must give way."

And well did British bravery deserve the proud encomium,
Which their enduring courage drew from the brave
Napoleon;
And when the close column of infantry came on the British
square,
Then the British gave one loud cheer which did rend the
air.

Then the French army pressed forward at Napoleon's
command,
Determined, no doubt, to make a bold stand;

Then Wellington cried, "Up Guards and break their ranks through,
And chase the French invaders from off the field of Waterloo!"

Then, in a moment, they were all on their feet,
And they met the French, sword in hand, and made them retreat;
Then Wellington in person directed the attack,
And at every point and turning the French were beaten back.

And the road was choked and encumbered with the dead;
And, unable to stand the charge, the French instantly fled,
And Napoleon's army of yesterday was now a total wreck,
Which the British manfully for ten long hours held in check.

Then, panic-struck, the French were forced to yield,
And Napoleon turned his charger's head, and fled from the field,
With his heart full of woe, no doubt—
Exclaiming, "Oh, Heaven! my noble army has met with a total rout!"

THE LOSS OF THE "VICTORIA"

Alas! Now o'er Britannia there hangs a gloom,
Because over 400 British Tars have met with a watery tomb;
Who served aboard the "Victoria," the biggest ship in the navy,
And one of the finest battleships that ever sailed the sea.

And commanded by Sir George Tyron, a noble hero bold,
And his name on his tombstone should be written in letters of gold;

For he was skilful in naval tactics, few men could with him
    cope,
And he was considered to be the nation's hope.

'Twas on Thursday, the twenty-second of June,
And off the coast of Syria, and in the afternoon,
And in the year of our Lord eighteen ninety-three,
That the ill-fated "Victoria" sank to the bottom of the sea.

The "Victoria" sank in fifteen minutes after she was
    rammed,
In eighty fathoms of water, which was smoothly calmed;
The monster war vessel capsized bottom uppermost,
And, alas, lies buried in the sea totally lost.

The "Victoria" was the flagship of the Mediterranean Fleet,
And was struck by the "Camperdown" when too close they
    did meet,
While practising the naval and useful art of war,
How to wheel and discharge their shot at the enemy afar.
Oh, Heaven! Methinks I see some men lying in their
    beds,
And some skylarking, no doubt, and not a soul dreads
The coming avalanche that was to seal their doom,
Until down came the mighty fabric of the engine room.

Then death leaped on them from all quarters in a moment,
And there were explosions of magazines and boilers rent;
And the fire and steam and water beat out all life;
But I hope the drowned ones are in the better world free
    from strife.

Sir George Tyron was on the bridge at the moment of the
    accident
With folded arms, seemingly quite content;
And seeing the vessel couldn't be saved he remained till
    the last,
And went down with the "Victoria" when all succour was
    past.

Methinks I see him on the bridge like a hero brave,
And the ship slowly sinking into the briny wave;
And when the men cried, "Save yourselves without delay,"
He told them to save themselves, he felt no dismay.

'Twas only those that leaped from the vessel at the first
    alarm,
Luckily so, that were saved from any harm
By leaping into the boats o'er the vessel's side,
Thanking God they had escaped as o'er the smooth water
    they did glide.

At Whitehall, London, mothers and fathers did call,
And the pitiful scene did the spectators' hearts appal;
But the most painful case was the mother of J. P. Scarlet,
Who cried, "Oh, Heaven, the loss of my son I'll never
    forget."

Oh, Heaven! Befriend the bereaved ones, hard is their fate,
Which I am sorry at heart to relate;
But I hope God in His goodness will provide for them,
Especially the widows, for the loss of their men.

Alas! Britannia now will mourn the loss of her naval com-
    mander,
Who was as brave as the great Alexander;
And to his honour be it fearlessly told,
Few men would excel this hero bold.

Alas! 'Tis sad to be buried in eighty fathoms of Syrian sea,
Which will hide the secret of the "Victoria" to all eternity;
Which causes Britannia's sorrow to be profound
For the brave British Tars that have been drowned.

THE DISASTROUS FIRE AT SCARBOROUGH

'Twas in the year of 1898, and on the 8th of June,
A mother and six children met with a cruel doom
In one of the most fearful fires for some years past—
And as the spectators gazed upon them they stood aghast.

The fire broke out in a hairdresser's, in the town of Scar-
    borough,
And as the fire spread it filled the people's hearts with
    sorrow;
But the police and the fire brigade were soon on the ground,
Then the hose and reel were quickly sent round.

Oh! it was horrible to see the flames leaping up all around,
While amongst the spectators the silence was profound,
As they saw a man climb out to the parapet high,
Resolved to save his life, or in the attempt to die!

And he gave one half frantic leap, with his heart full of woe,
And came down upon the roof of a public-house 20 feet
    below;
But, alas! he slipped and fell through the skylight,
And received cuts and bruises : oh, what a horrible sight!

He was the tenant of the premises, Mr Brookes,
And for his wife and family he enquires, with anxious looks,
But no one could tell him, it did appear,
And when told so adown his cheeks flowed many a tear.

He had been sleeping by himself on the second floor,
When suddenly alarmed, he thought he'd make sure,
And try to escape from the burning pile with his life,
And try and save his family and his wife.

The fire brigade played on the first floor with great speed,
But the flames had very inflammable fuel upon which to
    feed,

So that the fire spread with awful rapidity.
And in twenty minutes the building was doomed to the
fourth storey.

The firemen wrought with might and main,
But still the fire did on them gain,
That it was two hours before they could reach the second
floor,
The heat being so intense they could scarcely it endure.

And inside all the time a woman and six children were
there,
And when the firemen saw them, in amazement they did
stare;
The sight that met their eyes made them for to start—
Oh, Heaven! the sight was sufficient to rend the strongest
heart.

For there was Mrs Brookes stretched dead on the floor,
Who had fallen in trying her escape for to procure.
She was lying with one arm over her ten months old child,
And her cries for help, no doubt, were frantic and wild;
And part of her arm was burned off as it lay above
The child she was trying to shield, which shows a mother's
love.

For the baby's flesh was partly uninjured by the flames,
Which shows that the loving mother had endured great
pains;
It, however, met its death by suffocation,
And as the spectators gazed theron, it filled their hearts
with consternation.

The firemen acted heroically, without any dread,
And when they entered the back premises they found the
six children dead;
But Mr Brookes, 'tis said, is still alive,
And I hope for many years he will survive.

Oh, Heaven! it is cruel to perish by fire,
Therefore let us be watchful before to our beds we retire,
And see that everything is in safe order before we fall
    asleep,
And pray that God o'er us in the night watch will keep.

THE DEATH OF CAPTAIN WARD

'Twas about the beginning of the past century
Billy Bowls was pressed into the British Navy,
And conveyed on board the "Waterwitch" without delay,
Scarce getting time to bid farewell to the villagers of Fair-
    way.

And once on board the "Waterwitch" he resolved to do his
    duty,
And if he returned safe home he'd marry Nelly Blyth, his
    beauty,
And he'd fight for old England like a jolly British tar,
And the thought of Nelly Blyth would solace him during
    the war.

Poor fellow, he little thought what he had to go through,
But in all his trials at sea he never did rue;
No, the brave tar became reconciled to his fate,
And felt proud of his commander, Captain Ward the Great.

And on board the "Waterwitch" was Tom Riggles, his old
    comrade,
And with such a comrade he seldom felt afraid;
Because the stories they told each other made the time pass
    quickly away,
And made their hearts feel light and gay.

'Twas on a Sunday morning and clear to the view,
Captain Ward the attention of his men he drew;

"Look!" he cried, "There's two French men-of-war on our
    right,
Therefore prepare, my lads, immediately to begin the fight."

Then the "Waterwitch" was steered to the ship that was
    most near,
While every man resolved to sell their lives most dear;
But the French commander disinclined to engage in the
    fight,
And he ordered his men to put on a press of canvas and
    take to flight.

Then Captain Ward gave the order to fire,
Then Billy Bowls cried, "Now we'll get fighting to our
    hearts' desire";
And for an hour a running fight was maintained,
And the two ships of the enemy near upon the "Water-
    witch" gained.

Captain Ward walked the deck with a firm tread,
When a shot from the enemy pierced the ship, yet he felt no
    dread;
But with a splinter Bill Bowls was wounded on the left arm,
And he cried, "Death to the frog-eaters, they have done me
    little harm."

Then Captain Ward cried, "Fear not, my men, we will win
    the day,
Now, men, pour in a broadside without delay";
Then they sailed around the "St. Denis" and the "Glorie,"
And in their cabin windows they poured a deadly fire.

The effect on the two ships was tremendous to behold,
But the Frenchmen stuck to their guns with courage bold;
And the crash and din of artillery was deafening to the ear,
And the cries of the wounded men were pitiful to hear.

Then Captain Ward to his men did say,
"We must board the Frenchman without delay";

Then he seized his cutlass as he spoke,
And jumped on board the "St. Denis" in the midst of the
smoke.

Then Bill Bowls and Tom Riggles hastily followed him,
Then, hand to hand, the battle did begin;
And the men sprang upon their foe and beat them back,
And hauled down their colours and hoisted the Union Jack.

But the men on board the "St. Denis" fought desperately
hard,
And just as the "St. Denis" was captured a ball struck
Captain Ward
Right on the forehead, and he fell without a groan,
And for the death of Captain Ward the men did moan.

Then the first lieutenant who was standing near by,
Loudly to the men did cry,
"Come, men, and carry your noble commander below;
But there's one consolation, we have beaten the foe."

And thus fell Captain Ward in the prime of life,
But I hope he is now in the better world free from strife;
But, alas! 'tis sad to think he was buried in the mighty
deep,
Where too many of our brave seamen silently sleep.

McGONAGALL'S ODE TO THE KING

Oh! God, I thank Thee for restoring King Edward the
Seventh's health again,
And let all his subjects throughout the Empire say Amen;
May God guard him night and day,
At home and abroad, when he's far away.

May angels guard his bed at night when he lies down,
And may his subjects revere him, and on him do not frown;

May he be honoured by them at home and abroad,
And may he always be protected by the Eternal God.

My blessing on his noble form, and on his lofty head,
May all good angels guard him while living and when dead;
And when the final hour shall come to summons him away,
May his soul be wafted to the realms of bliss I do pray.

Long may he reign, happy and serene,
Also his Queen most beautiful to be seen;
And may God guard his family by night and day,
That they may tread in the paths of virtue and not go
    astray.

May God prosper King Edward the Seventh wherever he
    goes,
May he always reign victorious over his foes;
Long may he be spared to wear the British Crown,
And may God be as a hedge around him at night when he
    lies down;
May God inspire him with wisdom, and long may he reign
As Emperor of India and King Edward the VII.—Amen.

A SUMMARY HISTORY OF LORD CLIVE

About a hundred and fifty years ago,
History relates it happened so,
A big ship sailed from the shores of Britain
Bound for India across the raging main.

And many of the passengers did cry and moan
As they took the last look of their old home,
Which they were fast leaving far behind,
And which some of them would long bear in mind.

Among the passengers was a youth about seventeen years
    old,
Who had been a wild boy at home and very bold,

And by his conduct had filled his parents' hearts with
    woe,
Because to school he often refused to go.

And now that he was going far away from home,
The thought thereof made him sigh and groan,
For he felt very sad and dejected were his looks,
And he often wished he had spent more time at his
    books.

And when he arrived in India he searched for work there,
And got to be clerk in a merchant's office, but for it he
    didn't care;
The only pleasure he found was in reading books,
And while doing so, sad and forlorn were his looks.

One day while feeling unhappy he fired a pistol at his
    own head,
Expecting that he would kill himself dead;
But the pistol wouldn't go off although he tried every
    plan,
And he felt sorry, and resolved to become a better man.

So Clive left his desk and became a soldier brave,
And soon rose to be a captain and manfully did behave;
For he beat the French in every battle,
After all their foolish talk and prattle.

Then he thought he would take a voyage home to his
    friends,
And for his bad behaviour towards them he would make
    some amends;
For he hadn't seen them for many years,
And when he thought of them he shed briny tears.

And when he arrived in London
The people after him in crowds did run;
And they flocked to see him every minute,
Because they thought him the most famous man in it.

And all the greatest people in the land
Were proud to shake him by the hand;
And they gave him a beautiful sword because he had
    fought so well
And of his bravery the people to each other did tell.

And when his own friends saw him they to him ran,
And they hardly knew him, he looked so noble a man;
And his parents felt o'erjoyed when they saw him home
    again,
And when he left his parents again for India it caused
    them great pain.

But it was a good thing Clive returned to India again,
Because a wicked prince in his territory wouldn't allow
    the British to remain,
And he resolved to drive them off his land,
And marched upon them boldly with thousands of his
    band.

But the bad prince trembled when he heard that Clive
    had come,
Because the British at the charge of the bayonet made
    his army run;
And the bad prince was killed by one of his own band,
And the British fortunately got all his land.

And nearly all India now belongs to this country,
Which has been captured by land and by sea,
By some of the greatest men that ever did live,
But the greatest of them all was Robert Clive.

THE BATTLE OF THE NILE

'Twas on the 18th of August in the year of 1798,
That Nelson saw with inexpressible delight

The City of Alexandria crowded with the ships of France,
So he ordered all sail to be set, and immediately
   advance.

And upon the deck, in deep anxiety he stood,
And from anxiety of mind he took but little food;
But now he ordered dinner to be prepared without
   delay,
Saying, I shall gain a peerage to-morrow, or Westminster
   Abbey.

The French had found it impossible to enter the port of
   Alexandria,
Therefore they were compelled to withdraw;
Yet their hearts were burning with anxiety the war to
   begin,
But they couldn't find a pilot who would convey them
   safely in.

Therefore Admiral Brueys was forced to anchor in
   Aboukir Bay,
And in a compact line of battle, the leading vessels lay
Close to a shoal, along a line of very deep water,
There they lay, all eager to begin the murderous
   slaughter.

The French force consisted of thirteen ships of the line,
As fine as ever sailed on the salt sea brine;
Beside four Frigates carrying 1,196 guns in all,
Also 11,230 men as good as ever fired a cannon ball.

The number of the English ships were thirteen in all,
And carrying 1,012 guns, including great and small;
And the number of the men were 8,068,
All jolly British tars and eager for to fight.

As soon as Nelson perceived the position of the enemy,
His active mind soon formed a plan immediately;

As the plan he thought best, as far as he could see,
Was to anchor his ships on the quarter of each of the
    enemy.

And when he had explained his mode of attack to his
    officers and men,
He said, form as convenient, and anchor at the stern;
Then first gain the victory, and make the best use of it
    you can,
Therefore I hope every one here to-day, will do their
    duty to a man.

When Captain Berry perceived the boldness of the plan,
He said, my Lord, I'm sure the men will do their duty
    to a man;
And, my Lord, what will the world say, if we gain the
    victory?
Then Nelson replied, there's no if in the case, and that
    you'll see.

Then the British tars went to work without delay,
All hurried to and fro, making ready for the fray;
And there wasn't a man among them, but was confident
    that day,
That they would make the French to fly from Aboukir
    Bay.

Nelson's Fleet did not enter Aboukir Bay at once,
And by adopting that plan, that was his only chance;
But one after another, they bore down on the enemy;
Then Nelson cried, now open fire my heroes, immedia-
    tely!

Then the shores of Egypt trembled with the din of the
    war,
While sheets of flame rent the thick clouds afar;
And the contending fleets hung incumbent o'er the bay,
Whilst our British tars stuck to their guns without the
    least dismay.

And loudly roared the earthly thunder along the river
  Nile,
And the British ship Orion went into action in splendid
  style;
Also Nelson's Ship Vanguard bore down on the foe,
With six flags flying from her rigging high and low.

Then she opened a tremendous fire on the Spartiate,
And Nelson cried, fear not my lads we'll soon make them
  retreat!
But so terrific was the fire of the enemy on them,
That six of the Vanguards guns were cleared of men.

Yet there stood Nelson, the noble Hero of the Nile,
In the midst of death and destruction on deck all the
  while;
And around him on every side, the cannon balls did
  rattle,
But right well the noble hero knew the issue of the battle.

But suddenly he received a wound on the head,
And fell into the arms of Captain Berry, but fortunately
  not dead;
And the flow of blood from his head was very great,
But still the hero of the Nile was resigned to his fate.

Then to the Cockpit the great Admiral was carried down,
And in the midst of the dying, he never once did frown;
Nor he didn't shake with fear, nor yet did he mourn,
But patiently sat down to wait his own turn.

And when the Surgeon saw him, he instantly ran,
But Nelson said, Surgeon, attend to that man;
Attend to the sailor you were at, for he requires your aid,
Then I will take my turn, don't be the least afraid.

And when his turn came, it was found that his wound
  was but slight,
And when known, it filled the sailors' hearts with delight;

And they all hoped he would soon be able to command
    in the fight,
When suddenly a cry arose of fire! which startled Nelson
    with affright.

And unassisted he rushed upon the deck, and to his
    amaze,
He discovered that the Orient was all in a blaze;
Then he ordered the men to lower the boats, and relieve
    the enemy,
Saying, now men, see and obey my orders immediately.

Then the noble tars manned their boats, and steered to
    the Orient,
While the poor creatures thanked God for the succour
    He had sent;
And the burning fragments fell around them like rain,
Still our British tars rescued about seventy of them from
    the burning flame,

And of the thirteen sail of the French the British cap-
    tured nine,
Besides four of their ships were burnt, which made the
    scene sublime,
Which made the hero of the Nile cry out thank God
    we've won the day,
And defeated the French most manfully in Aboukir Bay.

Then the victory was complete and the French Fleet
    annihilated,
And when the news arrived in England the people's
    heart's felt elated,
Then Nelson sent orders immediately through the fleet,
That thanksgiving should be returned to God for the
    victory complete.

THE BATTLE OF CORUNNA

'Twas in the year of 1808, and the autumn of the year,
Napoleon resolved to crush Spain and Portugal without
   fear;
So with a mighty army three hundred thousand strong
Through the passes of the Pyrenees into Spain he passed
   along.

But Sir John Moore concentrated his troops in the north,
And into the west corner of Spain he boldly marched
   forth;
To cut off Napoleon's communications with France
He considered it to be advisable and his only chance.

And when Napoleon heard of Moore's coming, his march
   he did begin,
Declaring that he was the only General that could oppose
   him;
And in the month of December, when the hills were
   clad with snow,
Napoleon's army marched over the Guadiana Hills with
   their hearts full of woe.

And with fifty thousand cavalry, infantry, and artillery,
Napoleon marched on, facing obstacles most dismal to
   see;
And performed one of the most rapid marches recorded
   in history,
Leaving the command of his army to Generals Soult and
   Ney.

And on the 5th of January Soult made his attack,
But in a very short time the French were driven back;
With the Guards and the 50th Regiment and the 42nd
   conjoint,
They were driven from the village of Elnina at the
   bayonet's point.

Oh! it was a most gorgeous and inspiring sight
To see Sir John Moore in the thickest of the fight,
And crying aloud to the 42nd with all his might,
"Forward, my lads, and charge them with your bayonets
    left and right."

Then the 42nd charged them with might and main,
And the French were repulsed again and again;
And although they poured into the British ranks a
    withering fire,
The British at the charge of the bayonet soon made them
    retire.

Oh! that battlefield was a fearful sight to behold,
'Twas enough to make one's blood run cold
To hear the crack, crack of the musketry and the
    cannon's roar,
Whilst the dead and the dying lay weltering in their
    gore.

But O Heaven! it was a heartrending sight,
When Sir John Moore was shot dead in the thickest of
    the fight;
And as the soldiers bore him from the field they looked
    woebegone,
And the hero's last words were "Let me see how the
    battle goes on."

Then he breathed his last with a gurgling sound,
And for the loss of the great hero the soldiers' sorrow
    was profound,
Because he was always kind and served them well,
As they thought of him tears down their cheeks trickling
    fell.

Oh! it was a weird and pathetic sight
As they buried him in the Citadel of Corunna at the
    dead of night,

While his staff and men shed many tears
For the noble hero who had commanded them for many
    years.

Success to the British Army wherever they go,
For seldom they have failed to conquer the foe;
Long may the Highlanders be able to make the foe reel,
By giving them an inch or two of cold steel.

LITTLE PIERRE'S SONG

In a humble room in London sat a pretty little boy,
By the bedside of his sick mother her only joy,
Who was called Little Pierre, and whose father was dead;
There he sat poor boy, hungry and crying for bread.

There he sat humming a little song, which was his own,
But to the world it was entirely unknown,
And as he sang the song he felt heartsick,
But he resolved to get Madame Malibran to sing his
    song in public.

Then he paused for a moment and clasped his hands,
And running to the looking-glass before it he stands,
Then he smoothed his yellow curls without delay,
And from a tin box takes a scroll of paper worn and
    grey.

Then he gave one fond eager glance at his mother,
Trying hard brave boy his grief to smother,
As he gazed on the bed where she lay,
But he resolved to see Madame Malibran without delay.

Then he kissed his mother while she slept,
And stealthly from the house he crept,
And direct to Madame Malibran's house he goes,
Resolved to see her no matter who did him oppose.

And when he reached the door he knocked like a brave
    gallant
And the door was answered by her lady servant,
Then he told the servant Madame Malibran he wished
    to see
And the servant said, oh yes, I'll tell her immediately.

Then away the servant goes feeling quite confident,
And told her a little boy wished to see her just one
    moment
Oh! well, said Madame Malibran, with a smile,
'Fetch in the little boy he will divert me a while.

So Little Pierre was brought in with his hat under his
    arm
And in his hand a scroll of paper, thinking it no harm,
Then walked straight up to Madame Malibran without
    dread
And said, dear lady my mother is sick and in want of
    bread.

And I have called to see if you would sing my little song,
At some of your grand concerts, Ah! say before long,
Or perhaps you could sell it to a publisher for a small
    sum,
Then I could buy food for my mother and with it would
    run.
Then Madame Malibran rose from her seat most costly
    and grand
And took the scroll of paper from Pierre's hand
And hummed his little song, to a plaintive air,
Then said, your song is soul stirring I do declare.

Dear child did you compose the words she asked Pierre,
Oh yes my dear lady just as you see,
Well my dear boy I will sing your song to-night,
And you shall have a seat near me on the right.

Then Pierre, said, Oh! lady I cannot leave my mother,
But my dear boy, as for her you need not bother,
So dear child don't be the least cast down,
And in the meantime here is a crown.

And for your mother you can buy food and medicine,
So run away and be at the concert to-night in time
Then away he ran and bought many little necessary
    things
And while doing so his little song he hums and sings.

Then home to his poor sick mother he quickly ran,
And told her of his success with Madame Malibran,
Then his mother cried, Oh! Pierre, you are a very good
    boy,
And to hear of your success my heart is full of joy.

Dear mother, I am going to the concert hall to-night,
To hear Madame Malibran, which will my heart delight,
Oh! well said his mother, God speed you my little man,
I hope you will be delighted to hear Madame Malibran.

So to the concert hall he goes, and found a seat there,
And the lights and flashing of diamonds made him stare,
And caused a joyous smile to play upon his face,
For never had he been in so grand a place.

There the brave boy sat and Madame Malibran came at
    last
And with his eyes rivetted on her he stared aghast,
And to hear her sing, Oh! how he did long,
And he wondered if the lady would really sing his song.

At last the great singer commenced his little song,
And many a heart was moved and the plaudits loud and
    long
And as she sang it Pierre clapped his hands for joy.
That he felt as it were free from the world's annoy.

When the concert was over his heart felt as light as the
    air
And as for money now he didn't seem to care,
Since the great singer in Europe had sung his little song,
But he hoped that dame fortune would smile on him ere
    long.

The next day he was frightened by a visit from Madame
    Malibran
And turning to his mother, she said your little boy
    Madame
Will make a fortune for himself and you before long,
Because I've been offered a large sum for his little song.

And Madame thank God you have such a gifted son,
But dear Madame heavens will must be done,
Then Pierre knelt and prayed that God would the lady
    bless
For helping them in the time of their distress.

And the memory of Pierre's prayer made the singer do
    more good
By visiting the poor and giving them clothing and food
And Pierre lightened her last moments ere her soul fled
    away
And he came to be one of the most talented composers
    of the day.

THE CAPTURE OF LUCKNOW

'Twas near the Begum Kothie the battle began,
Where innocent blood as plentiful as water ran;
The Begum Kothie was a place of honour given to the
    93rd,
Which heroically to a man they soon did begird.

And the 4th Punjaub Rifles were their companions in
   glory,
And are worthy of their names enrolled in story,
Because they performed prodigious wonders in the fight,
By killing and scattering the Sepoys left and right.

The 93rd Highlanders bivouacked in a garden sur-
   rounded by mud walls,
Determined to capture the Begum Kothie no matter what
   befalls—,
A place strongly fortified and of enoromus strength,
And protected by strong earthworks of very great length.

And added to these obstacles was the most formidable of
   all—
A broad deep ditch that ran along the wall,
Which the storming party not even guessed at before;
But this barrier the British soon did climb o'er.

But early the next morning two batteries of Artillery
   were pounding away,
And the fight went on for the whole day;
And the defenders of the building kept up rattling
   musketry fire,
And when night fell the British had to retire.

Next day the contest was renewed with better success,
And the 93rd in all their beauty forward did press,
And moved on toward the position without firing a shot,
And under cover of some ruined buildings they instantly
   got.
And here for a few minutes they kept themselves under
   cover,
While each man felt more anxious than another
To attack the merciless rebels while it was day,
Because their blood was up and eager for the fray.

Still the enemy kept up a blazing fire at them pell-mell,
But they fired too high and not a man of them fell;

And the bullets whistled around them again and again,
Still on went the unwavering Highlanders with might
and main.

But when they reached the ditch they were taken by
surprise,
By the unexpected obstacle right before their eyes;
But Captain Middleton leapt into the ditch and showed
them the way,
And immediately the whole of the men were after him
without delay.

Leith Hay himself was among the first across,
And gained a footing on the other side without any
personal loss;
And he assisted in helping the rest out of the ditch,
While the din of the war was at the highest pitch.

'Twas then the struggle commenced in terrible earnest:
While every man was resolved to do his best;
And the enemy barricaded every entrance so as a single
man could only pass,
Determined to make a strong resistance, and the British
to harass.

But barrier after barrier soon was passed;
And the brave men no doubt felt a little harassed,
But they fought desperately and overturned their foes
at every point,
And put the rebels to flight by shot and bayonet conjoint.

The Sheiks and the Horse Guards behaved right well—
Because beneath their swords, by the score, the Sepoys
fell;
And their beautiful war steeds did loudly neigh and roar,
While beneath their hoofs they trampled them all o'er.

And as for John McLeod—the pipe-major of the 93rd,
He kept sounding his bagpipes and couldn't be stirred—

Because he remembered his duty in the turmoil,
And in the battlefield he was never known to recoil.

And as for Major General McBain—he was the hero in
the fight;
He fought heroically—like a lion— with all his might;
And again and again he was met by desperate odds,
But he scattered them around him and made them kiss
the sods.

And he killed eleven of the enemy with sword in hand,
Which secured for him the proudest of all honours in
the land,
Namely, that coveted honour called the Victoria Cross,
Of which many a deserving hero has known the loss.

And as for brave Hodson—he was a warrior born,
And military uniform did his body adorn;
And his voice could be heard in the battle afar,
Crying—"Come on my boys there is nothing like war!"

But, in a moment, a volley was discharged at him,
And he fell mortally wounded, while the Sepoys did
grin;
Then the Highlanders closed with their foes and made
them retreat,
And left them not till every rebel lay dead at their feet.

Then Sir Colin Campbell to his men did say,—
"Men, I feel proud that we have captured Lucknow this
day;
Therefore strike up the bagpipes and give one hearty
cheer,
And enjoy yourselves, my heroes, while ye are here."

THE BURNS STATUE
(A fragment)

This Statue, I must confess, is magnificent to see,
And I hope will long be appreciated by the people of
　　Dundee;
It has been beautifully made by Sir John Steell,
And I hope the pangs of hunger he will never feel.

This Statue is most elegant in its design,
And I hope will defy all weathers for a very long time;
And I hope strangers from afar with admiration will
　　stare
On this beautiful statue of thee, Immortal Bard of Ayr.

Fellow-citizens, this Statue seems most beautiful to the
　　eye,
Which would cause Kings and Queens for such a one to
　　sigh,
And make them feel envious while passing by
In fear of not getting such a beautiful Statue after they
　　die.

FAREWELL ADDRESS AT THE ARGYLE HALL,
TUESDAY, JUNE 22, 1880

Fellow Citizens of Dundee.
I now must bid farewell to ye.
For I am going to London far away.
But when I will return again I cannot say.

Farewell! Farewell! to the bonnie banks o' the Silvery
　　Tay.
Also the beautiful Hill o' Balgay.
And the ill fated Bridge o' the Silvery Tay.
Which I will remember when I am far away.

Farewell! to my friends and patrons all.
That rallied around me in the Music Hall.
And those that has rallied around me to-night,
I shall not forget when out of sight.

And if I ever return to Dundee again,
I hope it will be with the laurels of fame.
Plac'd on my brow by dame fortune that fickle Jade.
And to Court her favour I am not afraid.

Farewell! to every one in the Argyle Hall.
That has Come to hear McGonagall.
Recite, and sing, his Songs to-night.
Which I hope will long be remember'd when I'm out of
    sight.

Adieu to all my enemies that want to mock me when
    passing by.
But I excuse them for their ignorance and leave them
    to the most high.
And, once again, my friends, and enemies. I bid ye all
    good bye.
And when I am gone ye will for me heave a sigh: —

I return my thanks to my Chairman and my Committee,
For the Kindness they have always shown to me.
I hope the Lord! will protect them when I am far away.
And prosper them in all their undertakings by night and
    by day.

THE SUNDERLAND CALAMITY

'Twas in the town of Sunderland, and in the year of 1883,
That about 200 children were launch'd into eternity
While witnessing an entertainment in Victoria Hall,
While they, poor little innocents, to God for help did
    call.

The entertainment consisted of conjuring, and the ghost
  illusion play,
Also talking waxworks, and living marionettes, and given
  by Mr Fay;
And on this occasion, presents were to be given away,
But in their anxiety of getting presents they wouldn't
  brook delay,
And that is the reason why so many lives have been taken
  away;
But I hope their precious souls are in heaven to-day.

As soon as the children began to suspect
That they would lose their presents by neglect,
They rush'd from the gallery, and ran down the stairs
  pell-mell,
And trampled one another to death, according as they
  fell.

As soon the the catastrophe became known throughout
  the boro'
The people's hearts were brim-full of sorrow,
And parents rush'd to the Hall terror-stricken and wild,
And each one was anxious to find their own child.

Oh! it must have been a most horrible sight
To see the dear little children struggling with all their
  might
To get out at the door at the foot of the stair,
While one brave little boy did repeat the Lord's Prayer.

The innocent children were buried seven or eight layers
  deep,
The sight was heart-rending and enough to make one
  weep;
It was a most affecting spectacle and frightful to behold
The corpse of a little boy not above four years old,

Who had a top-coat on much too big for him,
And his little innocent face was white and grim,

And appearing to be simply in a calm sleep—
The sight was enough to make one's flesh to creep.

The scene in the Hall was heart-sickening to behold,
And enough to make one's blood run cold.
To see the children's faces, blackened, that were trampled
    to death,
And their parents lamenting o'er them with bated breath.

Oh! it was most lamentable for to hear
The cries of the mothers for their children dear;
And many mothers swooned in grief away
At the sight of their dead children in grim array.

There was a parent took home a boy by mistake,
And after arriving there his heart was like to break
When it was found to be the body of a neighbour's child;
The parent stood aghast and was like to go wild.

A man and his wife rush'd madly in the Hall,
And loudly in grief on their children they did call,
And the man searched for his children among the dead
Seemingly without the least fear or dread.
And with his finger pointing he cried. "That's one! two!
Oh! heaven above, what shall I do;"
And still he kept walking on and murmuring very low,
Until he came to the last child in the row;

Then he cried, "Good God! all my family gone
And now I am left to mourn alone;"
And staggering back he cried, "Give me water, give me
    water!"
While his heart was like to break and his teeth seem'd to
    chatter.

Oh, heaven! it must have been most pitiful to see
Fathers with their dead children upon their knee
While the blood ran copiously from their mouths and
    ears
And their parents shedding o'er them hot burning tears.

I hope the Lord will comfort their parents by night and
     by day,
For He gives us life and He takes it away,
Therefore I hope their parents will put their trust in
     Him,
Because to weep for dead it is a sin.

Her Majesty's grief for the bereaved parents has been
     profound,
And I'm glad to see that she has sent them £50;
And I hope from all parts of the world will flow relief
To aid and comfort the bereaved parents in their grief.

THE WRECK OF THE BARQUE "LYNTON" WHILE BOUND FOR ASPINWALL, HAVING ON BOARD 1000 TONS OF COAL

A sad tale of the sea, I will unfold,
About Mrs Lingard, that Heroine bold;
Who struggled hard in the midst of the hurricane wild,
To save herself from being drowned, and her darling
     child.

'Twas on the 8th of September, the Barque "Lynton"
     sailed for Aspinwall,
And the crew on board, numbered thirteen in all;
And the weather at the time, was really very fine,
On the morning that the ill-fated vessel left the Tyne.

And on the 19th of November, they hove in sight of
     Aspinwall,
But little did they think there was going to be a squall;
When all on a sudden, the sea came rolling in,
And a sound was heard in the heavens, of a rather
     peculiar din.

Then the vivid lightning played around them, and the
  thunder did roar,
And the rain came pouring down, and lashed the barque
  all o'er;
Then the Captain's Wife and Children were ordered
  below,
And every one on board began to run to and fro.

Then the hurricane in all its fury, burst upon them,
And the sea in its madness, washed the deck from stem
  to stem;
And the rain poured in torrents, and the waves seemed
  mountains high,
Then all on board the barque, to God for help, did
  loudly cry.

And still the wind blew furiously, and the darkness was
  intense,
Which filled the hearts of the crew with great suspense,
Then the ill-fated vessel struck, and began to settle down,
Then the poor creatures cried, God save us, or else we'll
  drown!

Then Mrs Lingard snatched to her breast, her darling
  child,
While loudly roared the thunder, and the hurricane wild;
And she cried, Oh! God of heaven, save me and my
  darling child,
Or else we'll perish in the hurricane wild.

'Twas then the vessel turned right over, and they were
  immersed in the sea,
Still the poor souls struggled hard to save their lives,
  most heroically;
And everyone succeeded in catching hold of the keel
  garboard streak,
While with cold and fright, their hearts were like to
  break.

Not a word or a shriek came from Mrs Lingard, the Captain's wife,
While she pressed her child to her bosom, as dear she loved her life;
Still the water dashed over them again and again,
And about one o'clock, the boy, Hall, began to complain.

Then Mrs Lingard put his cold hands into her bosom,
To warm them because with cold he was almost frozen,
And at the same time clasping her child Hilda to her breast,
While the poor boy Hall closely to her prest.

And there the poor creatures lay huddled together with fear,
And the weary night seemed to them more like a year,
And they saw the natives kindling fires on the shore,
To frighten wild animals away, that had begun to roar.

Still the big waves broke over them, which caused them to exclaim,
Oh! God, do thou save us for we are suffering pain;
But, alas, the prayers they uttered were all in vain,
Because the boy Hall and Jonson were swept from the wreck and never rose again.
Then bit by bit the vessel broke up, and Norberg was swept away,
Which filled the rest of the survivors' hearts with great dismay;
But at length the longed for morning dawned at last,
Still with hair streaming in the wind, Mrs Lingard to the wreck held fast.

Then Captain Lingard still held on with Lucy in his arms,
Endeavouring to pacify the child from the storms alarms;
And at last the poor child's spirits began to sink,
And she cried in pitiful accents, papa! papa! give me a drink.

And in blank amazement the Captain looked all round
    about,
And he cried Lucy dear I cannot find you a drink I
    doubt,
Unless my child God sends it to you,
Then he sank crying Lucy, my dear child, and wife,
    adieu! adieu!

'Twas then a big wave swept Lucy and the Carpenter
    away,
Which filled Mrs Lingard's heart with great dismay,
And she cried Mr Jonson my dear husband and child are
    gone,
But still she held to the wreck while the big waves rolled
    on.

For about 38 hours they suffered on the wreck,
At length they saw a little boat which seemed like a
    speck,
Making towards them on the top of a wave,
Buffeting with the billows fearlessly and brave.

And when the boat to them drew near,
Poor souls they gave a feeble cheer,
While the hurricane blew loud and wild,
Yet the crew succeeded in saving Mrs Lingard and her
    child.

Also, the Steward and two sailors named Christophers
    and Eversen,
Able-bodied and expert brave seamen.
And they were all taken to a French Doctor's and
    attended to,
And they caught the yellow fever, but the Lord brought
    them through.

And on the 6th of December they embarked on board
    the ship Moselle,
All in high spirits, and in health very well,

And arrived at Southampton on the 29th of December,
A day which the survivors will long remember.

THE GREAT YELLOW RIVER INUNDATION
IN CHINA

'Twas in the year of 1887, and on the 28th of September,
Which many people of Honan, in China, will long
    remember;
Especially those that survived the mighty deluge,
That fled to the mountains, and tops of trees, for refuge.

The river burst its embankments suddenly at dead of
    night,
And the rushing torrent swept all before it left and
    right;
All over the province of Honan, which for its fertility,
Is commonly called by historians, the garden of China.

The river was at its fullest when the embankment gave
    way,
And when the people heard it, oh! horror and dismay;
'Twas then fathers and mothers leaped from their beds
    without delay,
And some saved themselves from being drowned, but
    thousands were swept away.

Oh! it was a horrible and most pitiful scene,
To hear fathers and mothers and their children loudly
    scream;
As the merciless water encircled their bodies around,
While the water spirits laughed to see them drowned.

Oh! heaven, it must have been an appalling sight,
To witness in the dead stillness of the night

Frantic fathers and mothers, struggling hard against the
roaring flood,
To save themselves and little ones, their own flesh and
blood.

The watchmen tried to patch the breach, but it was all
in vain,
Because the banks were sodden with the long prolonged
rain;
And driven along by a high wind, which brought the
last strain,
Which caused the water with resistless fury to spread o'er
the plain.

And the torrent poured into the valley of the La Chia
river,
Sweeping thousands of the people before it ere a helping
hand could them deliver;
Oh! it was horrible to hear the crashing of houses fallen
on every side,
As the flood of rushing waters spread far and wide.

The Chinese offer sacrifices to the water spirits twice a
year,
And whether the water spirits of God felt angry I will
not aver;
But perhaps God has considered such sacrifices a sin,
And has drowned so many thousands of them for not
worshipping Him.

How wonderful are the works of God,
At times among His people abroad;
Therefore, let us be careful of what we do or say,
For fear God doth suddenly take our lives away.

The province of Honan is about half the size of Scotland,
Dotted over with about 3000 villages, most grand;
And inhabited by millions of people of every degree,
And these villages, and people were transformed into a
raging sea.

The deluge swept on over the fertile and well-cultivated
    land,
And the rushing of the mighty torrent no power could
    withstand;
And the appalling torrent was about twenty feet deep,
And with resistless fury everything before it it did sweep.

Methinks I see the waste of surging waters, and hear its
    deafening roar,
And on its surface I see corpses of men and women by
    the score;
And the merciless torrent in the darkness of the night,
Sportively tossing them about, oh! what a horrible
    sight.

Besides there were buffaloes and oxen, timber, straw and
    grain,
Also three thousand villages were buried beneath the
    waters of the plain;
And multitudes beneath their own roofs have found a
    watery grave,
While struggling hard, no doubt, poor souls their lives
    to save.

Therefore good people at home or abroad,
Be advised by me and trust more in God,
Than the people of Honan, the benighted Chinese,
For fear God punished you likewise for your iniquities.

THE DEATH OF FRED. MARSDEN
THE AMERICAN PLAYWRIGHT

A pathetic tragedy I will relate,
Concerning poor Fred. Marsden's fate,
Who suffocated himself by the fumes of gas,
On the 18th of May, and in the year of 1888, alas!

Fred. Marsden was a playwright, the theatrical world
knows
And was highly esteemed by the people, and had very
few foes;
And in New York, in his bedroom, he took his life away,
And was found by his servant William in his bedroom
where he lay.

The manner in which he took his life: first he locked the
door,
Then closed down the window, and a sheet to shreds he
tore,
And then stopped the keyholes and chinks through which
air might come,
Then turned on the single gas-burner, and soon the deed
was done.

About seven o'clock in the evening he bade his wife
good-night,
And she left him, smoking, in his room, thinking all was
right,
But when morning came his daughter said she smelled
gas,
Then William, his servant, called loudly on him, but no
answer, alas!

Then suspicion flashed across William's brain, and he
broke open the door,
Then soon the family were in a state of uproar,
For the room was full of gas, and Mr. Marsden quite
dead,
And a more kind-hearted father never ate of the world's
bread.

And by his kindness he spoiled his only child,
His pretty daughter Blanche, which made him wild;
For some time he thought her an angel, she was so very
civil,
But she dishonoured herself, and proved herself a devil.

Her father idolised her, and on her spared no expense,
And the kind-hearted father gave her too much indul-
gence,
Because evening parties and receptions were got up for
her sake,
Besides, he bought her a steam yacht to sail on Schroon
Lake.

His means he lavished upon his home and his wife,
And he loved his wife and daughter as dear as his life;
But Miss Blanche turned to folly, and wrecked their
home through strife,
And through Miss Marsden's folly her father took his life.

She wanted to ride, and her father bought her a horse,
And by giving her such indulgences, in morals she grew
worse;
And by her immoral actions she broke her father's heart;
And in my opinion, she has acted a very ungrateful part.

At last she fled from her father's house, which made him
mourn,
Then the crazy father went after her and begged her to
return,
But she tore her father's beard, and about the face beat
him,
Then fled to her companions in evil, and thought it no
sin.

Then her father sent her one hundred dollars, and found
her again,
And he requested her to come home, but it was all in
vain;
For his cruel daughter swore at him without any dread,
And, alas! next morning, he was found dead in his bed.

And soon theatrical circles were shocked to learn,
Of the sudden death of genial Fred. Marsden,

Whose house had been famous for its hospitality,
To artists, litterateurs, and critics of high and low degree.

And now dear Mrs Marsden is left alone to mourn
The loss of her loving husband, who to her will ne'er
　　return;
But I hope God will be kind to her in her bereavement,
And open her daughter's eyes, and make her repent

For being the cause of her father's death, the generous
　　Fred,
Who oft poor artists and mendicants has fed;
But, alas! his bounties they will never receive more,
Therefore poor artists and mendicants will his loss de-
　　plore.

Therefore, all ye kind parents of high and low degree,
I pray ye all, be advised by me,
And never pamper your children in any way,
Nor idolise them, for they are apt to go astray,

And treat ye, like pretty Blanche Marsden,
Who by her folly had been the death of one of the finest
　　men;
So all kind parents, be warned by me,
And remember always this sad Tragedy!

DEATH AND BURIAL OF LORD TENNYSON

Alas! England now mourns for her poet that's gone—
The late and the good Lord Tennyson.
I hope his soul has fled to heaven above,
Where there is everlasting joy and love.

He was a man that didn't care for company,
Because company interfered with his study,
And confused the bright ideas in his brain,
And for that reason from company he liked to abstain.

He has written some fine pieces of poetry in his time,
Especially the May Queen, which is really sublime;
Also the gallant charge of the Light Brigade—
A most heroic poem, and beautifully made.

He believed in the Bible, also in Shakespeare,
Which he advised young men to read without any fear;
And by following the advice of both works therein,
They would seldom or never commit any sin.

Lord Tennyson's works are full of the scenery of his
    boyhood,
And during his life all his actions were good;
And Lincolnshire was closely associated with his history,
And he has done what Wordsworth did for the Lake
    Country.

His remains now rest in Westminster Abbey,
And his funeral was very impressive to see;
It was a very touching sight, I must confess,
Every class, from the Queen, paying a tribute to the
    poet's greatness.

The pall-bearers on the right of the coffin were Mr W.
    E. H. Lecky,
And Professor Butler, Master of Trinity, and the Earl of
    Rosebery;
And on the left were Mr J. A. Froude and the Marquis
    of Salisbury,
Also Lord Selborne, which was an imposing sight to see.

There were also on the left Professor Jowett,
Besides Mr Henry Whyte and Sir James Paget,
And the Marquis of Dufferin and the Duke or Argyll,
And Lord Salisbury, who seemed melancholy all the
    while.

The chief mourners were all of the Tennyson family,
Including the Hon. Mr and Mrs Hallam Tennyson and
    Masters Lionel and Aubrey,

And Mr Arthur Tennyson, and Mr and Mrs Horatio
    Tennyson;
Also Sir Andrew Clark, who was looking woe begone.

The bottom of the grave was thickly strewn with white
    roses,
And for such a grave kings will sigh where the poet now
    reposes;
And many of the wreaths were much observed and
    commented upon,
And conspicuous amongst them was one from Mrs Glad-
    stone.

The Gordon boys were there looking solemn and serene,
Also Sir Henry Ponsonby to represent the Queen;
Likewise Henry Irving, the great tragedian,
With a solemn aspect, and driving his brougham.

And, in conclusion, I most earnestly pray,
That the people will erect a monument for him without
    delay,
To commemorate the good work he has done,
And his name in gold letters written thereon!

A NEW YEAR'S RESOLUTION TO LEAVE DUNDEE

Welcome! thrice welcome! to the year 1893,
For it is the year that I intend to leave Dundee,
Owing to the treatment I receive,
Which does my heart sadly grieve.
Every morning when I go out
The ignorant rabble they do shout
'There goes Mad McGonagall'
In derisive shouts, as loud as they can brawl,
And lifts stones and snowballs, throws them at me;
And such actions are shameful to be heard in the City of
    Dundee.

And I'm ashamed, kind Christians, to confess,
That from the Magistrates I can get no redress.
Therefore I have made up my mind, in the year of 1893,
To leave the Ancient City of Dundee,
Because the citizens and me cannot agree.
The reason why?—because they disrespect me,
Which makes me feel rather discontent.
Therefore, to leave them I am bent;
And I will make my arrangements without delay,
And leave Dundee some early day.

LINES IN REPLY TO THE BEAUTIFUL POET, WHO WELCOMED NEWS OF McGONAGALL'S DEPARTURE FROM DUNDEE

Dear Johnny, I return my thanks to you;
But more than thanks is your due
For publishing the scurrilous poetry about me
Leaving the Ancient City of Dundee.

The rhymster says, we'll weary for your schauchlin'
      form;
But if I'm not mistaken I've seen bonnier than this in a
      field of corn;
And, as I venture to say and really suppose,
His form seen in a cornfield would frighten the crows.

But, dear Johnny, as you said, he's just a lampoon,
And as ugly and as ignorant as a wild baboon;
And, as far as I can judge or think,
He is a vendor of strong drink.

He says my nose would make a peasemeal warrior weep;
But I've seen a much bonnier sweep,
And a more manly and wiser man
Than he is by far, deny it who can!

And, in conclusion, I'd have him to beware,
And never again to interfere with a poet's hair,
Because Christ the Saviour wore long hair,
And many more good men, I do declare.

Therefore I laugh at such bosh that appears in print.
So I hope from me you will take the hint,
And never publish such bosh of poetry again,
Or else you'll get the famous *Weekly News* a bad name.

LINES IN MEMORIAM REGARDING THE ENTERTAINMENT I GAVE ON THE 31st MARCH, 1893, IN REFORM STREET HALL, DUNDEE

'Twas on the 31st of March, and in the year of 1893,
I gave an entertainment in the city of Dundee,
To select a party of gentlemen, big and small,
Who appreciated my recital in Reform Street Hall.

The meeting was convened by J. P. Smith's manager, High Street,
And many of J. P. Smith's employees were there me to greet,
And several other gentlemen within the city,
Who were all delighted with the entertainment they got from me.

Mr Green was the chairman for the night,
And in that capacity he acted right;
He made a splendid address on my behalf,
Without introducing any slang or chaff.

I wish him success during life;
May he always feel happy and free from strife,
For the kindness he has ever shown to me
During our long acquaintance in Dundee.

I return my thanks to Mr J. P. Smith's men,
Who were at my entertainment more than nine or ten;
And the rest of the gentlemen that were there,
Also deserves my thanks, I do declare.

Because they showered upon me their approbation,
And got up for me a handsome donation,
Which was presented to me by Mr Green,
In a purse most beautiful to be seen.

Which was a generous action in deed,
And came to me in time of need.
And the gentlemen that so generously treated me
I'll remember during my stay in Dundee.

LINES IN PRAISE OF MR J. GRAHAM HENDERSON, HAWICK

Success to Mr J. Graham Henderson, who is a good man,
And to gainsay it there's few people can,
I say so from my own experience,
And experience is a great defence.

He is a good man, I venture to say,
Which I declare to the world without dismay,
Because he's given me a suit of Tweeds, magnificent to
   see,
So good that it cannot be surpassed in Dundee.

The suit is the best of Tweed cloth in every way,
And will last me for many a long day;
It's really good, and in no way bad,
And will help to make my heart feel glad.

He's going to send some goods to the World's Fair,
And I hope of patronage he will get the biggest share;

Because his Tweed cloth is the best I ever did see,
In the year of our Lord eighteen hundred and ninety-
three.

At the International Exhibition, and the Isle of Man
Exhibition,
He got a gold medal for each, in recognition
Of his Scotch Tweeds, so good and grand,
Which cannot be surpassed in fair Scotland.

Therefore, good people, his goods are really grand,
And manufactured at Weensforth Mill, Hawick, Scot-
land;
Where there's always plenty of Tweeds on hand,
For the ready cash at the people's command.

Mr Tocher measured me for the suit,
And it is very elegant, which no one will dispute,
And I hope Mr Henry in Reform Street
Will gain customers by it, the suit is so complete.

A TRIBUTE TO DR MURISON

Success to the good and skilful Dr Murison,
For golden opinions he has won
From his patients one and all,
And from myself, McGonagall.

He is very skilful and void of pride;
He was so to me when at my bedside,
When I turned badly on the 25th of July,
And was ill with inflammation, and like to die.

He told me at once what was ailing me;
He said I had been writing too much poetry,
And from writing poetry I would have to refrain,
Because I was suffering from inflammation on the brain.

And he has been very good to me in my distress,
Good people of Dundee, I honestly confess,
And to all his patients as well as me
Within the Royal city of Dundee.

He is worthy of the public's support,
And to his shop they should resort
To get his advice one and all;
Believe me on him ye ought to call.

He is very affable in temper and a skilful man,
And to cure all his patients he tries all he can;
And I wish him success for many a long day,
For he has saved me from dying, I venture to say;
The kind treatment I received surpasses all
Is the honest confession of McGonagall.

THE KESSACK FERRY-BOAT FATALITY

'Twas on Friday the 2nd of March in the year of 1894,
That the Storm Fiend did loudly laugh and roar
Along the Black Isle and the Kessack Ferry shore,
Whereby six men were drowned, which their friends will
    deplore.

The accident is the most serious that has occurred for
    many years,
And their relatives no doubt will shed many tears,
Because the accident happened within 200 yards of the
    shore,
While Boreas he did loudly rail and roar.

The ferry-boat started from the north or Black Isle,
While the gusty gales were blowing all the while
From the south, and strong from the south-west,
And to get to land the crew tried their utmost best.

The crew, however, were very near the land,
When the gusts rose such as no man could withstand,
With such force that the ferry-boat flew away
From her course, down into the little bay,

Which opens into the Moray Firth and the river Ness,
And by this time the poor men were in great distress,
And they tried again and again to get back to the pier,
And to save themselves from being drowned they began
    to fear.

And at last the poor men began to despair,
And they decided to drop anchor where they were,
While the Storm Fiend did angry roar,
And the white-crested billows did lash the shore.

And the water poured in, but was baled out quickly,
And the men's clothes were wet, and they felt sickly,
Because they saw no help in the distance,
Until at last they blew the fog-horn for assistance.

And quickly in response to their cry of distress,
Four members of the coastguard, in coastguard dress,
Whose station overlooked the scene, put off in a small
    boat,
And with a desperate struggle they managed to keep her
    afloat.

Then the coastguards and boat drifted rapidly away,
Until they found themselves in the little bay,
Whilst the big waves washed o'er them, again and again,
And they began to think their struggling was all in vain.

But they struggled on manfully until they came upon a
    smaller boat,
Which they thought would be more easily kept afloat,
And to which the hawser was soon transferred,
Then for a second time to save the ferrymen all was
    prepared.

Then the coastguards drifted down alongside the ferry-
    boat,
And with great difficulty they kept themselves afloat,
Because the big waves were like mountains high,
Yet the coastguards resolved to save the ferrymen or
    die.

Then at last the ferrymen got into the coastguard boat,
And they all toiled manfully to keep her afloat,
Until she was struck as she rose on the crest of the wave,
Then each one tried hard his life to save.

And the poor men's hearts with grief were rent,
For they were thrown into the merciless sea in a moment,
And out of the eight men two have been saved,
All owing to their swimming abilities, and how they
    behaved.

Oh! it must have been a fearful sight,
To see them striving hard with all their might
To save themselves from a watery grave,
While the Storm Fiend did laugh and angry did rave.

SAVING A TRAIN

A poor old woman lived on the line of the Ohio Railway,
Where the train passed near by night and day:
She was a widow, with only one daughter,
Who lived with her in a log-hut near a deep gorge of
    water.

Which was spanned o'er from ridge to ridge,
By a strong metal railway bridge;
And she supported herself by raising and selling poultry,
Likewise eggs and berries, in great variety.

She often had to walk to the nearest town,
Which was many miles, but she seldom did frown;
And there she sold her basket of produce right quickly,
Then returned home with her heart full of glee.

The train passed her hut daily to the town.
And the conductor noticed her on the line passing down,
So he gave her a lift, poor soul, many a time,
When he chanced to see her travelling along the line.

The engineman and brakesman to her were very good,
And resolved to help her all they could;
And thought they were not wronging the railway
          company
By giving the old woman a lift when she felt weary.

And, by thinking so, they were quite right,
For soon an accident occurred in the dead of night,
Which filled the old woman's heart with fright,
When she heard the melted torrents of snow descending
    in the night.

Then the flood arose, and the railway bridge gave way
With a fearful crash and plash,—Oh, horror and dismay!
And fell into the seething and yawning gulf below,
Which filled the old woman's heart with woe.

Because in another half-hour the train would be due,
So the poor old woman didn't know what to do;
And the rain fell in a flood, and the wind was howling,
And the heavens above seemed angry and scowling.

And alas! there was no telegraph along the line,
And what could she do to warn the train in time,
Because a light wouldn't live a moment in the rain,
But to save the train she resolved to strain every vein.

Not a moment was to be lost, so to work she went,
And cut the cords of her bed in a moment;

Then shouldered the side-pieces and head-pieces in all,
Then shouted to her daughter to follow as loud as she
    could bawl.

Then they climbed the step embankment, and there fear-
    lessly stood,
And piled their furniture on the line near the roaring
    flood,
And fired the dry combustibles, which blazed up bright,
Throwing its red light along the line a weird-like sight.

Then the old woman tore her red gown from her back,
And tying it to the end of a stick she wasn't slack;
Then ran up the line, waving it in both hands,
While before, with a blazing chair-post, her daughter
    stands.

Then round a curve the red eye of the engine came at
    last,
While the poor old woman and her daughter stood
    aghast;
But, thank God, the engine stopped near the roaring
    fire,
And the train was saved, as the old woman did desire.

And such an old woman is worth her weight in gold,
For saving the train be it told;
She was a heroine, true and bold,
Which should be written on her tombstone in letters of
    gold.

BEAUTIFUL BALMERINO

Beautiful Balmerino on the bonnie banks of Tay,
It's a very bonnie spot in the months of June and May;
The scenery there is changing and fascinating to see,
Especially the surroundings of the old Abbey,

187

Which is situated in the midst of trees on a rugged hill,
Which visitors can view at their own free will;
And the trees and shrubberies are lovely to view,
Especially the trees on each side of the avenue

Which leads up to the Abbey amongst the trees;
And in the summer time it's frequented with bees,
And also crows with their unmusical cry,
Which is a great annoyance to the villagers that live
near by.

And there in the summer season the mavis sings,
And with her charming notes the woodland rings;
And the sweet-scented zephyrs is borne upon the gale,
Which is most refreshing and invigorating to inhale.

Then there's the stately Castle of Balmerino
Situated in the midst of trees, a magnificent show,
And bordering on the banks o' the silvery Tay,
Where visitors can spend a happy holiday.

As they view the castle and scenery around
It will help to cheer their spirits I'll be bound;
And if they wish to view Wormit Bay
They can walk along the braes o' the silvery Tay.

THE BATTLE OF OMDURMAN

Ye Sons of Great Britain! come join with me
And sing in praise of the gallant British Armie,
That behaved right manfully in the Soudan,
At the great battle of Omdurman.

'Twas in the year of 1898, and on the 2nd of September,
Which the Khalifa and his surviving followers will long
remember,

Because Sir Herbert Kitchener has annihilated them out-
　　right,
By the British troops and Soudanese in the Omdurman
　　fight.

The Sirdar and his Army left the camp in grand array,
And marched on to Omdurman without delay,
Just as the brigades had reached the crest adjoining the
　　Nile,
And became engaged with the enemy in military style.

The Dervishes had re-formed under cover of a rocky
　　eminence,
Which to them, no doubt, was a strong defence,
And they were massed together in battle array
Around the black standard of the Khalifa, which made a
　　grand display.

But General Maxwell's Soudanese brigade seized the
　　eminence in a short time,
And General Maxwell's Soudanese brigade then joined
　　the firing line;
And in ten minutes, long before the attack could be
　　driven home,
The flower of the Khalifa's army was almost overthrown.

Still manfully the dusky warriors strove to make head-
　　way,
But the Soudanese troops and British swept back with-
　　out dismay,
And their main body were mown down by their deadly
　　fire—
But still the heroic Dervishes refused to retire.

And defiantly they planted their standards and died by
　　them,
To their honour be it said, just like brave men;
But at last they retired, with their hearts full of woe,
Leaving the field white with corpses, like a meadow
　　dotted with snow.

The chief heroes in the fight were the 21st Lancers;
They made a brilliant charge on the enemy with ringing
    cheers,
And through the dusky warriors' bodies their lances they
    did thrust,
Whereby many of them were made to lick the dust.

Then at a quarter past eleven the Sirdar sounded the
    advance,
And the remnant of the Dervishes fled, which was their
    only chance,
While the cavalry cut off their retreat while they ran;
Then the Sirdar, with the black standard of the Khalifa,
    headed for Omdurman.

And when the Khalifa saw his noble army cut down,
With rage and grief he did fret and frown;
Then he spurred his noble steed, and swiftly it ran,
While inwardly to himself he cried, "Catch me if you
    can!"

And Mahdism now has received a crushing blow,
For the Khalifa and his followers have met with a com-
    plete overthrow;
And General Gordon has been avenged, the good Chris-
    tian,
By the defeat of the Khalifa at the battle of Omdurman.

Now since the Khalifa has been defeated and his rule at
    an end,
Let us thank God that fortunately did send
The brave Sir Herbert Kitchener to conquer that bad
    man,
The inhuman Khalifa, and his followers at the battle of
    Omdurman.

Success to Sir Herbert Kitchener! he is a great com-
    mander,
And as skilful in military tactics as the great Alexander,

Because he devised a very wise plan,
And by it has captured the town of Omdurman.

I wish success to the British and Soudanese Army,
May God protect them by land and by sea,
May he enable them always to conquer the foe,
And to establish what's right wherever they go.